THE EMPIRIC **MBA**

THE EMPIRIC
MBA

LESSONS FROM 101 BUSINESS LEGENDS

Uncover the secrets of success from Founders, CEOs and Experts

MIKE VERMILION

Copyright © 2024. All rights reserved.

No part of this book may be reproduced in any form or by any electronic or mechanical means, including information storage and retrieval systems, without permission in writing from the publisher. The only exception is by a reviewer, who may quote short excerpts in a published review.

ISBN: 979-8345472293

Table of Contents

QUICKSTART 9
FOUNDERS & CEOs 13
    Abigail Johnson 14
    Andrew Jassy 16
    Anita Roddick 18
    Arianna Huffington 20
    Bill Gates 22
    Bob Iger 24
    Brian Chesky 26
    Cathie Wood 28
    Coco Chanel 30
    Daniel Ek 32
    Dara Khosrowshahi 34
    Elon Musk 36
    Eric Schmidt 38
    Estée Lauder 40
    Henry Ford 42
    Howard Schultz 44
    Indra Nooyi 46
    Jack Bogle 48
    Jack Ma 50
    Jamie Dimon 52
    Jane Fraser 54
    Jeff Bezos 56
    Jensen Huang 58
    Larry Fink 60
    Larry Page 62
    Lisa Su 64
    Marc Benioff 66
    Marillyn Hewson 68

Marissa Mayer ... 70
Mark Zuckerberg ... 72
Mary Barra ... 74
Meg Whitman ... 76
Melanie Perkins ... 78
Michael Bloomberg ... 80
Michael Dell ... 82
Oprah Winfrey ... 84
Phil Knight ... 86
Reed Hastings ... 88
Richard Branson ... 90
Rosalind Brewer ... 92
Sara Blakely ... 94
Satya Nadella ... 96
Sergey Brin ... 98
Sheryl Sandberg ... 100
Steve Jobs ... 102
Sundar Pichai ... 104
Susan Wojcicki ... 106
Tim Cook ... 108
Walt Disney ... 110
Warren Buffett ... 112

AUTHORS & EXPERTS ... 115

Amy Edmondson ... 116
Brendon Burchard ... 118
Brian Tracy ... 120
Cal Newport ... 122
Carol Dweck ... 124
Charles Duhigg ... 126
Chris Voss ... 128
Clayton Christensen ... 130
Dale Carnegie ... 132
Daniel Kahneman ... 134

Daniel Pink	136
Darren Hardy	138
Dave Ramsey	140
David Allen	142
Edward de Bono	144
Eric Ries	146
Gary Vaynerchuk	148
Grant Cardone	150
Gretchen Rubin	152
Hal Elrod	154
Harold Kerzner	156
Ivan Misner	158
James Clear	160
Jeanne Bliss	162
John C. Maxwell	164
Keith Ferrazzi	166
Laura Vanderkam	168
Leo Babauta	170
Marie Kondo	172
Michael Hyatt	174
Michael Porter	176
Nancy Duarte	178
Nassim Nicholas Taleb	180
Nick Murray	182
Peter Drucker	184
Peter Senge	186
Philip Kotler	188
Porter Gale	190
Ramit Sethi	192
Robert Kiyosaki	194
Robin Sharma	196
Roger Fisher	198
Seth Godin	200
Simon Sinek	202

Stephen Covey 204
Suze Orman 206
Tim Brown 208
Tim Ferriss 210
Tony Hsieh 212
Tony Robbins 214
Zig Ziglar 216

A HEARTFELT THANK YOU 219

QUICKSTART

Dream big. Start small. Act now.

— ROBIN SHARMA

Welcome!

In a world where business education often begins in the classroom, the true lessons of success are learned in the trenches of real-world experience. While a formal MBA—Master of Business Administration—might teach you the theories of management, the formulas of finance, and the structures of strategy, the most profound insights into business success come from the lives and minds of those who have not just studied these principles but lived them.

Welcome to *THE EMPIRIC MBA*. This book is not merely a collection of biographies or a compilation of famous quotes. It is a practical roadmap to prosperity, drawn from the lived experiences of 101 of the most iconic figures in business. Here, you will find the condensed wisdom of founders who turned ideas into empires, CEOs who steered companies through both calm and storm, and experts who have dedicated their lives to mastering the essential skills that drive performance.

Why This Book?

In today's fast-paced and ever-evolving business landscape, the path to achievement is less about following a prescribed set of rules and more about navigating the complexities of human experience, intuition, and decision-making. Conventional education provides a foundation, but it is the empirical knowledge—the lessons learned from the actual journey—that shapes the most successful leaders.

This book was born out of a simple yet profound question: What can we learn from those who have walked the path before us? To answer this, I've brought together the voices of 101 individuals who have achieved extraordinary success and left indelible marks on the world. Their stories are as diverse as their backgrounds, but they share common threads of resilience, innovation, and an unrelenting drive to turn vision into reality.

The Blueprint

To make the wisdom of these 101 legends as accessible and impactful as possible, they are divided into two groups:

FOUNDERS & CEOs — Visionaries who started with a dream and built global brands from the ground up. Leaders who excelled in the art of guiding companies through challenges, growth, and transformation.

AUTHORS & EXPERTS — Specialists dedicated to mastering and teaching the critical skills needed in today's competitive landscape. From innovation and leadership to productivity, communication, sales, and many others.

Within each group, the personalities are listed alphabetically, with no particular order of importance. Each entry presents a concise biography that captures the essence of the individual's career and achievements, followed by their most inspirational quotes with direct applications to business. This structure allows you to easily navigate the book, whether you're just seeking random inspiration from time to time or journeying through each chapter from cover to cover.

Along the way, as a bonus, you'll also discover an incredible collection of references to other must-read books on personal and professional development.

The Power of Stories and Quotes

Why pair biographies with quotes? Because stories give context, and quotes distill the essence of those stories into memorable, actionable insights. A single sentence can encapsulate years of experience, a moment of clarity, or a defining decision that altered the course of history.

In this book, each biography is accompanied by quotes that reflect the individual's core beliefs and guiding principles, providing a window into their mindset. These aren't just any quotes. They are words that have inspired action, sparked revolutions in industries, and shaped the destinies of companies. They are the mantras that these leaders returned to time and again, guiding them through their most challenging moments and propelling them to their greatest triumphs.

Whether you are an aspiring entrepreneur, an established business leader, or simply someone passionate about understanding what drives success, this book is designed to be your companion. As you turn the pages, you'll discover that there is no single path to greatness. Instead, there are countless routes, each as unique as the individual who walked it. Through their words and experiences, you'll find inspiration, guidance, and perhaps the spark you need to embark on your own journey.

The Journey Begins Here

The world of business is vast, complex, and endlessly fascinating. But at its core, it is driven by people—individuals with vision, passion, and the courage to defy the odds. As you immerse yourself in the stories and wisdom of these iconic personalities, remember that each of them started where you are now: with a dream, a desire to make an impact, and the willingness to learn, adapt, and grow.

This is not just a book. It is an invitation to learn from the best, to incorporate their wisdom, and to apply their lessons to your own life. The journey of 101 business legends begins now, and through their stories, you might just find the keys to unlocking your own potential.

Welcome to *THE EMPIRIC MBA*. Let the journey begin.

FOUNDERS & CEOs

Be courageous. It's one of the only places left uncrowded.

— ANITA RODDICK

Abigail Johnson

(CEO of Fidelity Investments)

Abigail Johnson (born 1961) is a prominent business leader and the CEO of Fidelity Investments, one of the largest asset management firms in the world. Born in Boston, Massachusetts, Johnson is the granddaughter of Edward C. Johnson II, the founder of Fidelity. She earned a degree in art history from Hobart and William Smith Colleges before pursuing an MBA from Harvard Business School. Johnson joined Fidelity in 1988 as an analyst and gradually worked her way up through the ranks.

Her most significant achievement came in 2014 when she became CEO of Fidelity Investments, succeeding her father, Edward C. "Ned" Johnson III. Under her leadership, Fidelity has expanded its offerings in digital assets and sustainable investing, maintaining its position as a leader in financial services. Johnson's focus on innovation and customer-centric strategies has helped the company adapt to the rapidly changing economic landscape.

In addition to her role at Fidelity, Johnson has strongly advocated diversity and inclusion within the financial industry. She is one of the most powerful women in finance, known for her strategic insight and commitment to advancing the role of women in business. Johnson's leadership continues to shape the future of Fidelity and the broader investment world.

Success requires persistence, resilience, and the ability to see challenges as opportunities.
—*CNBC, 2019*

Don't assume that someone else knows what they're doing and that you don't. It's one of the biggest mistakes you can make.
—*CNN Money, 2017*

Leadership isn't about having all the answers. It's about asking the right questions.
—*Fortune Most Powerful Women Summit, 2016*

The more you invest in knowledge, the better equipped you'll be to handle the ups and downs of the business world.
—*Forbes, 2016*

Success in business is not a destination, but an ongoing process of growth, improvement, and adaptation.
—*Forbes, 2017*

The future belongs to those who understand the opportunities of change.
—*Fortune, 2018*

Innovation requires taking risks, and not every idea is going to succeed. That's okay, as long as you're learning from your failures and trying again.
—*Forbes, 2016*

When you believe that you can be the best, you do things differently.
—*Bloomberg Businessweek, 2015*

— ABIGAIL JOHNSON

Andrew Jassy

(CEO of Amazon)

Andrew Jassy (born 1968) is the CEO of Amazon, having taken over from Jeff Bezos in 2021. Jassy joined Amazon in 1997 after earning his MBA from Harvard Business School and was instrumental in building Amazon Web Services (AWS) from the ground up. Under his leadership, AWS, launched in 2006, grew to become the world's largest cloud computing platform, transforming the way businesses store and access data.

Jassy's leadership of AWS helped Amazon diversify its business and become a global leader in cloud services, powering companies like Netflix, Airbnb, and NASA. AWS remains one of Amazon's most profitable divisions, driving much of the company's overall success. His strategic insight into the growing importance of cloud computing revolutionized the tech industry, making Amazon a dominant force.

As Amazon's CEO, Jassy continues to guide the company through its next growth phase, focusing on areas like e-commerce, artificial intelligence, and logistics. Known for his customer-first mindset and strong operational skills, Jassy is regarded as one of the most influential tech leaders. He has a track record of identifying and capitalizing on emerging trends that have reshaped modern business practices.

One of the things I've learned is to make sure you're not overly dependent on a single person's opinion, even if that person is you.
—*The Wall Street Journal, 2020*

There's no compression algorithm for experience.
—*AWS re:Invent Keynote, 2015*

Speed matters in business—faster businesses are more successful.
—*AWS re:Invent Keynote, 2020*

Leaders have to be decisive and willing to make bold bets.
—*AWS re:Invent Keynote, 2019*

Invention requires two things: the ability to try a lot of experiments and not having to be right all the time.
—*AWS re:Invent Keynote, 2019*

You need to be relentlessly focused on what's most important to your customers.
—*AWS re:Invent Keynote, 2018*

The way to drive large impact and transformation is through experimentation and iteration.
—*AWS re:Invent Keynote, 2017*

If you want to be innovative, you have to be willing to fail.
—*The Verge, 2019*

Don't let the fear of change stop you from seizing opportunities for growth.
—*Business Insider, 2021*

— ANDREW JASSY

Anita Roddick

(Founder of The Body Shop)

Anita Roddick (1942–2007) was a British businesswoman and social activist who founded The Body Shop, a global cosmetics company known for its ethical approach to business. Born in Littlehampton, England, Roddick worked as a teacher before opening her first Body Shop in 1976. Inspired by her travels and a desire to provide natural, environmentally-friendly beauty products, she offered alternatives to mainstream cosmetics, emphasizing reusable packaging and cruelty-free ingredients.

Under Roddick's leadership, The Body Shop proliferated, becoming a worldwide chain with thousands of stores. She was a pioneer in promoting corporate social responsibility, using her platform to advocate for environmental sustainability, fair trade, and human rights. Roddick's activism was integral to the brand's identity, challenging traditional business models by proving that a company could be both profitable and principled.

Roddick's influence extended beyond her business. She was a vocal campaigner for numerous social causes, including Greenpeace and Amnesty International. Her unwavering commitment to ethical consumerism and dedication to making a positive impact on the world continue to inspire entrepreneurs and activists alike. Through her work, Roddick left a lasting legacy in both the business world and the broader movement for social justice.

Book Title

Be courageous. It's one of the only places left uncrowded.
—*The Independent*, 2007

If you think you're too small to have an impact, try going to bed with a mosquito.
—*Business as Unusual*, 2000

The business of business should not just be about money. It should be about responsibility. It should be about public good, not private greed.
—*Business as Unusual*, 2000

To succeed, you have to believe in something with such a passion that it becomes a reality.
—*Business as Unusual*, 2000

Entrepreneurs are outsiders by nature, outsiders with a work ethic. The most successful entrepreneurs are not driven by profit, they are driven by a passion to create.
—*Business as Unusual*, 2000

Nobody talks of entrepreneurship as survival, but that's exactly what it is and what nurtures creative thinking.
—*The Guardian*, 2005

If you do things well, do them better. Be daring, be first, be different, be just.
—*Business as Unusual*, 2000

I believe that business is the most powerful force for positive social change on the planet, and that anything is possible through ethical enterprise.
—*Business as Unusual*, 2000

— ANITA RODDICK

Arianna Huffington

(Co-founder of The Huffington Post)

Arianna Huffington (born 1950) is a prominent author, entrepreneur, and media mogul best known for founding The Huffington Post. Originally from Greece, she moved to the UK to study at Cambridge University, where she became the first foreign-born president of the Cambridge Union. Her early career was marked by her work as an author, writing several books on politics and culture, establishing her as a notable figure in media circles.

In 2005, Huffington launched The Huffington Post, an online news and blog site that not only became a cultural phenomenon but also significantly impacted the media landscape. The platform combined traditional news with a wide array of blog contributions, pioneering a new approach to digital media. Under her leadership, the site expanded rapidly, winning a Pulitzer Prize in 2012 and being acquired by AOL in 2011 for $315 million.

After stepping down from The Huffington Post in 2016, Huffington focused on health and wellness, founding Thrive Global, a company dedicated to ending the stress and burnout epidemic. Through her work, she continues to influence conversations around well-being, productivity, and the intersection of technology and human potential.

Book Title

Live life as though everything is rigged in your favor.
—*Thrive, 2014

We think, mistakenly, that success is the result of the amount of time we put in at work, instead of the quality of that time.
—*Thrive, 2014

Fearlessness is like a muscle. I know from my own life that the more I exercise it, the more natural it becomes to not let my fears run me.
—Inc., 2013

The difference between success and failure is not the absence of failure, it's the persistence through failure.
—*Thrive, 2014

The fastest way to break the cycle of perfectionism and become a fearless person is to give up the idea of doing it perfectly.
—*On Becoming Fearless, 2006

We need to accept that we won't always make the right decisions, that we'll screw up royally sometimes.
—Forbes, 2013

There is nothing like the feeling of being fully charged, fully alive, fully present.
—*The Sleep Revolution, 2016

Success is not about money or power, but about living a life you can be proud of.
—Time Magazine, 2014

— ARIANNA HUFFINGTON

Bill Gates

(Co-founder and former CEO of Microsoft)

Bill Gates (born 1955) is an American business magnate, software developer, and philanthropist best known as the co-founder of Microsoft Corporation. Raised in Seattle, Gates developed an early interest in computing, which led him to drop out of Harvard University in 1975 to start Microsoft with his childhood friend, Paul Allen. Microsoft quickly became a dominant force in the personal computing industry with the release of MS-DOS and, later, the Windows operating system, which became the global standard for PCs.

Gates' leadership at Microsoft was characterized by aggressive business strategies and a focus on innovation, which helped the company grow into one of the world's most valuable and influential tech firms. Beyond software, Gates played a crucial role in shaping the broader technology landscape, impacting everything from the development of the internet to the proliferation of personal computing.

In 2008, Gates transitioned from his day-to-day role at Microsoft to focus on philanthropy through the Bill & Melinda Gates Foundation, which he co-founded with his then-wife Melinda in 2000. The foundation has since become one of the largest private charitable organizations in the world, focusing on global health, education, and poverty alleviation, significantly expanding Gates' impact beyond the tech industry.

*Book Title

It's fine to celebrate success, but it is more important to heed the lessons of failure.
—*Harvard University Commencement Speech, 2007*

Your most unhappy customers are your greatest source of learning.
—**Business @ the Speed of Thought, 1999*

We always overestimate the change that will occur in the next two years and underestimate the change that will occur in the next ten. Don't let yourself be lulled into inaction.
—**The Road Ahead, 1995*

As we look ahead into the next century, leaders will be those who empower others.
—*Speech at Microsoft Conference, 1999*

Technology is just a tool. In terms of getting the kids working together and motivating them, the teacher is the most important.
—*ABC's Good Morning America, 2000*

If you show people the problems and you show them the solutions, they will be moved to act.
—*TED Talk: Innovating to Zero!, 2010*

We always need to think about how we can continue to evolve our processes and technology to do more with less.
—**Business @ the Speed of Thought, 1999*

Expectations are a form of first-class truth: If people believe it, it's true.
—*Wired, 1996*

— BILL GATES

Bob Iger

(CEO of The Walt Disney Company)

Bob Iger (born 1951) is an influential American business executive known for leading The Walt Disney Company as CEO. Raised in Long Island, New York, Iger began his career in media at ABC, where he climbed the ranks to become president of ABC Entertainment. When Disney acquired ABC in 1996, Iger transitioned into Disney's leadership team, eventually becoming its CEO in 2005.

Under Iger's leadership, Disney experienced tremendous growth, notably through strategic acquisitions that expanded the company's reach and influence. He orchestrated Disney's acquisitions of Pixar (2006), Marvel (2009), Lucasfilm (2012), and 21st Century Fox (2019), greatly enhancing Disney's content library and positioning it as a dominant force in entertainment. Iger also spearheaded the development of Disney+, a streaming service that quickly became a major player in the industry.

Iger is credited with modernizing Disney's approach to content and distribution while preserving its core values. His vision and ability to identify key opportunities helped Disney become one of the world's largest and most successful media companies. Iger is a prominent figure in the business world whose leadership style emphasizes innovation, collaboration, and long-term vision.

Book Title

The heart and soul of a company is creativity and innovation.
—*The Ride of a Lifetime, 2019

The riskiest thing we can do is just maintain the status quo.
—The Wall Street Journal, 2017

Don't be in the business of playing it safe. Be in the business of creating possibilities for greatness.
—*The Ride of a Lifetime, 2019

A company's culture is shaped by its leaders, and it defines the work experience and expectations of all employees.
—Harvard Business Review, 2018

Optimism is a great strategy. You have to believe that something great can come from all adversity.
—*The Ride of a Lifetime, 2019

Take responsibility when you screw up. Don't be defensive. Don't be arrogant. Apologize.
—*The Ride of a Lifetime, 2019

Long shots aren't usually as long as they seem.
—*The Ride of a Lifetime, 2019

You can't allow tradition to get in the way of innovation. There's a need to respect the past, but it's a mistake to revere your past.
—The New York Times, 2019

If you can dream it, you can do it. But it's up to you to make it happen.
—Business Insider, 2019

— BOB IGER

Brian Chesky

(Co-founder and CEO of Airbnb)

Brian Chesky (born 1981) is an American entrepreneur best known as the co-founder and CEO of Airbnb, the online marketplace that revolutionized the travel and hospitality industry. Born in New York, Chesky studied industrial design at the Rhode Island School of Design, where he developed a passion for user experience and design thinking, skills that would later become crucial to Airbnb's success.

In 2008, Chesky and his co-founders Joe Gebbia and Nathan Blecharczyk launched Airbnb as a platform for renting out air mattresses in their apartment to attendees of a design conference. What began as a modest idea soon evolved into a global phenomenon, allowing millions of hosts to rent their homes or rooms to travelers, transforming how people experience accommodations. Chesky's focus on community and building trust between users helped propel the platform to unprecedented growth.

Under Chesky's leadership, Airbnb has grown into a multi-billion-dollar company with a presence in over 190 countries. His innovative approach has reshaped how people think about travel and created a new economy of short-term rentals. Chesky continues to push the boundaries of business and technology, emphasizing design, trust, and global community in the company's mission.

Whatever you do, you should have a mission that you are prepared to sacrifice almost everything for.
—*Fast Company, 2017*

Build something 100 people love, not something 1 million people kind of like.
—*Forbes, 2015*

Don't do things that can be replicated. Do things that can't be replicated.
—*Fast Company, 2017*

You have to think about what your users want and how to make it better for them.
—*The New York Times, 2017*

I think the best companies are built by people who are passionate about something. If you don't have passion, you don't have energy. If you don't have energy, you have nothing.
—*Inc., 2016*

If we tried to think of a good idea, we wouldn't have been able to think of a good idea. You just have to find the solution for a problem in your own life.
—*Business Insider, 2014*

The stuff that matters in life is no longer stuff. It's other people. It's relationships. It's experience.
—*The Atlantic, 2016*

You will face rejection and failure in your life, but the most important thing is to bounce back stronger.
—*Inc., 2017*

— BRIAN CHESKY

Cathie Wood

(Founder and CEO of ARK Invest)

Cathie Wood (born 1955) is an influential American investor and the founder of ARK Invest, a firm specializing in disruptive innovation. Wood graduated from the University of Southern California with a degree in economics and finance. She began her career at Capital Group and later held senior roles at Jennison Associates and Alliance-Bernstein before launching ARK Invest in 2014.

Wood gained prominence for her bold investment strategy, focusing on high-growth sectors like artificial intelligence, electric vehicles, and genomics. Her approach set ARK Invest apart, mainly through the success of the ARK Innovation ETF, which attracted widespread attention due to its performance. She became known for predicting major trends in tech and innovation, such as early investments in Tesla and cryptocurrency.

Cathie Wood's leadership at ARK Invest has made her a high-profile figure in finance, primarily as she advocates for long-term investment in transformative technologies. Her forward-thinking philosophy and willingness to challenge traditional investing norms have earned her a reputation as one of the most dynamic leaders in the world of finance.

The best way to predict the future is to invest in it.
—*ARK Invest Webinar, 2020*

In investing, you need conviction. You need to have a point of view that the market doesn't appreciate yet.
—*CNBC, 2021*

Innovation is key to growth, and investing in innovation is the key to long-term success.
—*Forbes, 2020*

The time to invest in innovation is during uncertainty and fear.
—*CNBC, 2020*

Disruptive innovation is often underappreciated because it challenges the status quo.
—*ARK Invest Podcast, 2019*

You need to be willing to think differently and not be afraid to go against the crowd.
—*ARK Invest Podcast, 2019*

Investing is about understanding the future and being willing to invest in change.
—*CNBC, 2020*

Markets often fail to appreciate the magnitude of change that technology will bring.
—*Bloomberg, 2019*

Innovation is inherently controversial, but the rewards of understanding it early are extraordinary.
—*CNBC, 2021*

— CATHIE WOOD

Coco Chanel

(Founder of Chanel)

Coco Chanel (1883–1971) was a pioneering French fashion designer who revolutionized women's fashion in the 20th century. Born Gabrielle Bonheur Chanel in Saumur, France, she was raised in an orphanage after her mother's death, where she learned to sew. Chanel began her career as a milliner in Paris before opening her first boutique in 1910. Her designs broke away from the restrictive styles of the time, introducing comfortable yet elegant clothing emphasizing simplicity and freedom of movement.

Chanel's most iconic contribution was the little black dress, which became a symbol of timeless elegance. She also popularized the use of jersey fabric for women's clothing, previously used only for men's underwear. In 1921, she launched Chanel No. 5, the first perfume to bear a designer's name, which remains one of the best-selling fragrances in history. Chanel's use of menswear elements and her emphasis on understated luxury forever changed how women dressed.

Beyond fashion, Chanel built a brand that epitomized sophistication and independence. Her influence extended far beyond clothing, as she redefined femininity and helped shape modern fashion. Even after her death, the House of Chanel remains a dominant force in the fashion industry, embodying her legacy.

Book Title

Success is often achieved by those who don't know that failure is inevitable.
—*The Gospel According to Coco Chanel, 2009*

The most courageous act is still to think for yourself. Aloud.
—*Coco Chanel, 2010*

In order to be irreplaceable, one must always be different.
—*Chanel, 1998*

Don't spend time beating on a wall, hoping to transform it into a door.
—*The Gospel According to Coco Chanel, 2009*

There are people who have money and people who are rich.
—*The Gospel According to Coco Chanel, 2009*

Simplicity is the keynote of all true elegance.
—*The Gospel According to Coco Chanel, 2009*

I don't care what you think about me. I don't think about you at all.
—*Coco Chanel, 2010*

Fashion changes, but style endures.
—*Coco Chanel, 2015*

I invented my life by taking for granted that everything I did not like would have an opposite, which I would like.
—*Coco Chanel, 2010*

Luxury must be comfortable, otherwise it is not luxury.
—*The Gospel According to Coco Chanel, 2009*

— COCO CHANEL

Daniel Ek

(Co-founder and CEO of Spotify)

Daniel Ek (born 1983) is a Swedish entrepreneur best known as the co-founder and CEO of Spotify, the world's largest music streaming service. Ek began his career in technology at a young age, starting his first company at 14. After working with various tech startups, including the popular file-sharing service uTorrent, Ek saw an opportunity to revolutionize the music industry.

In 2006, alongside Martin Lorentzon, Ek launched Spotify, a platform to combat music piracy by offering users a legal and convenient way to access music. Under Ek's leadership, Spotify quickly gained popularity for its user-friendly interface and extensive music library, ultimately reshaping how people consume music globally. The company went public in 2018, marking a significant milestone in its growth.

Beyond Spotify, Ek is also known for his investments in technology startups and his advocacy for entrepreneurship. His vision for Spotify has transformed the music industry and set a new standard for digital content distribution. Ek continues to lead Spotify as it expands into new markets and explores innovations in podcasting and other forms of audio content. His work exemplifies the power of technology to disrupt traditional industries and create new business models.

There's no shortcut to success. You have to work hard and put in the effort day after day.
—*Business Insider, 2017*

The only way to do great work is to love what you do.
—*Wired, 2012*

Culture is the most important thing to get right. It's the foundation for any company's success.
—*Forbes, 2014*

To succeed in a startup, you have to be prepared to fail fast and learn quickly.
—*Inc., 2015*

You need to have a long-term perspective and not be afraid to disrupt your own business model.
—*Harvard Business Review, 2015*

You can't do anything great without a great team.
—*Business Insider, 2017*

Don't think about competition. Think about how you can make your product better than anyone else's.
—*The New York Times, 2015*

The biggest challenge is to stay focused. It's to have the discipline when there are so many competing priorities.
—*Fortune, 2016*

To build something truly impactful, you need to have a vision that goes beyond just making money.
—*The Wall Street Journal, 2018*

— DANIEL EK

Dara Khosrowshahi

(CEO of Uber)

Dara Khosrowshahi (born 1969) is an Iranian-American businessman best known as Uber's CEO. Raised in a family that fled Iran during the revolution, Khosrowshahi studied electrical engineering at Brown University before entering the world of finance. He started his career at Allen & Company and later transitioned into the travel industry as CFO of IAC, where he played a pivotal role in acquiring Expedia.

In 2005, Khosrowshahi became Expedia's CEO, expanding the company's global presence and significantly growing its market share. Under his leadership, Expedia acquired major travel brands like Orbitz and Travelocity, making it one of the world's largest online travel companies. His success at Expedia demonstrated his ability to scale and lead large, complex organizations.

In 2017, Khosrowshahi took the helm at Uber, a company embroiled in controversy at the time. He implemented significant changes to improve Uber's corporate culture and worked to steer the company toward profitability. He also oversaw Uber's initial public offering (IPO) in 2019, cementing his reputation as a capable leader in turbulent times. Khosrowshahi continues to focus on expanding Uber's services beyond ridesharing, aiming to turn it into a global transportation and delivery platform.

Success is about making a real difference in people's lives.
—*Fortune, 2019*

You have to have a constant push to innovate, to grow, and to think bigger.
—*CNBC, 2018*

You are only as good as the people you hire.
—*Business Insider, 2019*

If you're not building a culture that's responsive to the market, then you're going to lose.
—*The Wall Street Journal, 2018*

If you want to make something great, you have to work through setbacks and failures.
—*Uber All-Hands Meeting, 2018*

Building trust is more important than any short-term gain.
—*Bloomberg, 2020*

Customer obsession is key. You have to keep improving to stay relevant.
—*Recode, 2019*

Agility is the most important competitive advantage in today's fast-paced world.
—*Fast Company, 2019*

Change is inevitable, and those who embrace it will succeed.
—*CNBC, 2018*

— DARA KHOSROWSHAHI

Elon Musk

(Founder of SpaceX and CEO of Tesla)

Elon Musk (born 1971) is a visionary entrepreneur known for his transformative contributions to technology and space exploration. Born in Pretoria, South Africa, Musk showed an early interest in computing, teaching himself programming by age 12. He moved to the United States to study at the University of Pennsylvania, where he earned degrees in physics and economics. After a brief stint in a PhD program at Stanford, he left to pursue a career in business during the internet boom.

Musk co-founded Zip2, an online city guide software company, which he sold for nearly $300 million in 1999. He then created X.com, an online payment company that eventually became PayPal, acquired by eBay in 2002. Musk's entrepreneurial vision further expanded with the founding of SpaceX in 2002, a company focused on reducing space transportation costs to enable the colonization of Mars. SpaceX achieved numerous milestones, including the first privately funded spacecraft to reach orbit and successful crewed missions to the International Space Station.

In addition to SpaceX, Musk is the CEO and product architect of Tesla, Inc., which revolutionized the electric vehicle industry. His other ventures include Neuralink, focusing on brain-computer interfaces, and The Boring Company, which aims to reduce urban traffic through underground tunnels. Musk's relentless drive for innovation has made him one of the most influential figures in modern technology and business.

Great companies are built on great products.
—*Wired*, 2008

When something is important enough, you do it even if the odds are not in your favor.
—*60 Minutes*, 2014

Failure is an option here. If things are not failing, you are not innovating enough.
—*South by Southwest*, 2013

The first step is to establish that something is possible; then probability will occur.
—*Wired*, 2012

I think it is possible for ordinary people to choose to be extraordinary.
—*CNN*, 2011

Brand is just a perception, and perception will match reality over time.
—*Forbes*, 2012

If you get up in the morning and think the future is going to be better, it is a bright day. Otherwise, it's not.
—*Rolling Stone*, 2017

The single best piece of advice: Constantly think about how you could be doing things better and questioning yourself.
—*Entrepreneur*, 2012

I could either watch it happen or be a part of it.
—*Wired*, 2007

— ELON MUSK

Eric Schmidt

(Former CEO of Google)

Eric Schmidt (born 1955) is an American technologist and businessman renowned for his pivotal role in shaping Google into a global powerhouse. With a background in electrical engineering and computer science, Schmidt began his career at Xerox's Palo Alto Research Center (PARC) and later held leadership positions at Sun Microsystems and Novell. His profound expertise in technology and management made him a sought-after leader in Silicon Valley.

In 2001, Schmidt joined Google as CEO, at the behest of founders Larry Page and Sergey Brin, to provide seasoned leadership for the rapidly growing company. During his decade-long tenure as CEO, Schmidt oversaw Google's transformation from a search engine into a multi-faceted tech giant, launching products like Google Maps, Gmail, and Android. His strategic vision and operational expertise helped Google scale globally and solidify its position as a leader in the tech industry.

After stepping down as CEO in 2011, Schmidt served as Google's Executive Chairman and later as Chairman of Alphabet, Google's parent company. His contributions have left a lasting impact on the tech world, significantly influencing how information is accessed and shared globally. Beyond Google, Schmidt is known for his philanthropic efforts and work in artificial intelligence and national security.

Innovation is the key to growth, and technology is at the heart of innovation.
—*McKinsey Quarterly*, 2008

You need to fail, you need to take risks. You need to have the expectation that innovation is a process of failure.
—*The Wall Street Journal*, 2009

The best way to predict the future is to invent it.
—*Speech at Stanford University*, 2012

We run this company on questions, not answers.
—*The New York Times*, 2010

Every company that has achieved real scale has found a way to harness the creativity and energy of the people who work there.
—*Harvard Business Review*, 2014

The characteristic of great innovators and great companies is they see a space that others do not.
—*Fortune*, 2010

The future belongs to those who can take the next big idea and turn it into reality.
—*Web Summit*, 2014

In a world where everything is connected, everyone needs to have a voice.
—*Business Insider*, 2013

Sometimes disruption is what's needed to find a new way forward.
—*The Economist*, 2011

— ERIC SCHMIDT

Estée Lauder

(Co-founded Estée Lauder Companies)

Estée Lauder (1908–2004) was an American businesswoman who co-founded the Estée Lauder Companies, a leading global cosmetics brand. Born in Queens, New York, to Hungarian and Czech immigrant parents, she was introduced to the skincare world by her chemist uncle. In 1946, she launched her business with her husband, Joseph Lauder, starting with just four products. Lauder's focus on high-quality ingredients and personalized customer service set her apart in a competitive market.

One of her most significant achievements was the creation of the "gift with purchase" marketing strategy, which became a hallmark in the beauty industry. Her relentless commitment to innovation and brand prestige helped her company expand globally, establishing iconic brands such as Clinique, Aramis, and MAC under the Estée Lauder umbrella. She was also a pioneer in marketing, famously believing in the power of word-of-mouth and personal touch.

Lauder's influence extended beyond product innovation. She was a powerful force in branding and luxury marketing, with her products becoming synonymous with elegance and exclusivity. By the time of her passing, the Estée Lauder Companies had become a multi-billion-dollar empire with a presence in over 150 countries, leaving a legacy in the beauty industry.

Book Title

I never dreamed about success. I worked for it.
—*Business Week*, 1985

When you stop talking, you've lost your customer.
—*Business Builders in Cosmetics*, 1986

If you don't sell, it's not the product that's wrong, it's you.
—*Time Magazine*, 1998

I believed in my product. I could see that my competitors were selling the same creams under different names, but my creams were different.
—*Estée: A Success Story*, 1985

I have never worked a day in my life without selling. If I believe in something, I sell it, and I sell it hard.
—*Time Magazine*, 1998

You can't be afraid to fail. It's the only way you succeed—you're not going to succeed all the time, and I know that.
—*The New York Times*, 1999

Trust your instincts: if you have a gut feeling about something, listen to it.
—*Business Week*, 1985

I didn't have a formal education. I had something better: I worked hard.
—*Time Magazine*, 1998

Beauty is an attitude. There's no secret. Why do some people look better than others? It's attitude.
—*Estée: A Success Story*, 1985

— ESTÉE LAUDER

Henry Ford

(Founder of Ford Motor Company)

Henry Ford (1863–1947) was an American industrialist who revolutionized the automobile industry and mass production. Born in Dearborn, Michigan, Ford was fascinated by machinery from a young age. He founded the Ford Motor Company in 1903, and by 1908, he introduced the Model T, a car that became wildly popular due to its affordability and reliability. However, Ford's real innovation was the development of the moving assembly line in 1913, drastically reducing production time and costs.

Ford's assembly line method allowed the Model T to be produced in large quantities, making automobiles accessible to the average American. By 1918, half of all cars in the United States were Model T. Ford's impact wasn't limited to manufacturing. He also implemented the $5 workday, doubling wages and reducing working hours, which helped create a loyal workforce and a new middle class with the purchasing power to buy the cars they produced.

Beyond automobiles, Ford pioneered vertical integration, controlling every aspect of production from raw materials to finished product. His innovations in manufacturing and labor practices not only transformed the automotive industry but also had a profound influence on the development of modern industrial society, shaping the way we produce and consume goods to this day.

Book Title

Whether you think you can, or you think you can't – you're right.
—*Ford News, 1923*

Coming together is a beginning, staying together is progress, and working together is success.
—*Reader's Digest, 1953*

The only real mistake is the one from which we learn nothing.
—*Today and Tomorrow, 1926*

Failure is simply the opportunity to begin again, this time more intelligently.
—*My Life and Work, 1922*

Obstacles are those frightful things you see when you take your eyes off your goal.
—*The Forbes Scrapbook, 1950*

It is not the employer who pays the wages. Employers only handle the money. It is the customer who pays the wages.
—*Ford Ideals, 1922*

You can't build a reputation on what you are going to do.
—*The Book of Business Wisdom, 1997*

Nothing is particularly hard if you divide it into small jobs.
—*My Life and Work, 1922*

Quality means doing it right when no one is looking.
—*Ford Motor Company, 2003*

— HENRY FORD

Howard Schultz

(Former CEO of Starbucks)

Howard Schultz (born 1953) is an American businessman best known for transforming Starbucks into a global coffee powerhouse. Raised in a working-class family in Brooklyn, New York, Schultz attended Northern Michigan University on a football scholarship, where he earned a degree in communications. His early career included roles at Xerox and Hammarplast, where he first encountered Starbucks, a small coffee bean retailer in Seattle.

In 1982, Schultz joined Starbucks as Director of Retail Operations and Marketing. After a trip to Italy, where the coffee culture inspired him, he envisioned Starbucks as a "third place" between home and work. In 1987, Schultz acquired Starbucks with the help of investors and began expanding the company, introducing the coffeehouse concept to the U.S. and, eventually, the world. Under his leadership, Starbucks grew from 11 stores to over 30,000 globally, becoming synonymous with premium coffee and unique customer experience.

Schultz's tenure at Starbucks was marked by innovation and a solid commitment to social responsibility, including employee benefits and ethical sourcing initiatives. He stepped down as CEO in 2018 but remains influential in business and philanthropy, advocating for social change and exploring new ventures. His visionary approach to brand building and corporate responsibility defines Schultz's legacy.

Book Title

In times of adversity and change, we really discover who we are and what we're made of.
—*The New York Times, 2008*

When you're surrounded by people who share a passionate commitment around a common purpose, anything is possible.
—**Onward, 2011*

Risk more than others think is safe. Dream more than others think is practical.
—*Forbes, 2009*

When we began Starbucks, what I wanted to try to do was to create a set of values, guiding principles, and culture.
—*CNBC, 2014*

I think if you're an entrepreneur, you've got to dream big, and then dream bigger.
—*Forbes, 2013*

We can't be in the business of nostalgia. We have to create the future.
—*The Seattle Times, 2017*

You must find something that you deeply love and are passionate about and are willing to sacrifice a lot to achieve.
—*Forbes, 2010*

You can't build any kind of organization if you're not going to surround yourself with people who have experience and skill base beyond your own.
—**Pour Your Heart Into It, 1997*

— HOWARD SCHULTZ

Indra Nooyi

(Former CEO of PepsiCo)

Indra Nooyi (born 1955) is an Indian-American business leader renowned for her transformative leadership as the CEO of PepsiCo. Raised in Chennai, India, Nooyi earned her bachelor's degree from Madras Christian College and an MBA from the Indian Institute of Management Calcutta before moving to the United States to attend Yale School of Management. Her career began with roles at Johnson & Johnson and Boston Consulting Group, where she honed her strategic acumen.

In 1994, Nooyi joined PepsiCo, where her vision and strategic thinking quickly became evident. She was instrumental in reshaping the company's focus, advocating for healthier products and spearheading the acquisition of Tropicana and the merger with Quaker Oats, which brought Gatorade into PepsiCo's portfolio. In 2006, she became the CEO, a role she held for 12 years, during which she led the company through significant growth while emphasizing sustainable practices and corporate responsibility.

Nooyi's tenure at PepsiCo was marked by her commitment to "Performance with Purpose", balancing financial success with social responsibility. She is widely celebrated for her leadership and consistently ranks among the world's most powerful women. After stepping down as CEO in 2018, Nooyi continues to influence global business and advocate for women's empowerment and education.

Leadership is hard to define and good leadership even harder. But if you can get people to follow you to the ends of the earth, you are a great leader.
—*World Economic Forum, 2009*

Whatever anybody says or does, assume positive intent. You will be amazed at how your whole approach to a person or problem becomes very different.
—*The Wall Street Journal, 2008*

The one thing I have learned as a CEO is that leadership at various levels is vastly different. As you move up the organization, the requirements for leading that organization don't grow vertically, they grow exponentially.
—*Harvard Business Review, 2013*

If you want to improve the organization, you have to improve yourself, and the organization gets pulled up with you.
—*PepsiCo Leadership Meeting, 2010*

When you look at the world, the most successful people are those who have the passion for what they're doing. The bigger the passion, the more impactful the work.
—*Fortune, 2017*

Performance with purpose is not only about what we do; it is also about how we do it.
—*PepsiCo Annual Report, 2010*

The best way to do great work is to find what's most important to you and then do it in a way that taps into your strengths and your passions.
—*Commencement speech at University of North Carolina, 2015*

— INDRA NOOYI

Jack Bogle

(Founder of Vanguard Group)

Jack Bogle (1929-2019) was a legendary investor and the founder of The Vanguard Group, known for revolutionizing the investment industry by introducing the first index mutual fund available to retail investors. Born in Montclair, New Jersey, Bogle graduated from Princeton University, where his senior thesis laid the groundwork for his innovative approach to low-cost investing. His belief in the power of passive investing would go on to shape the financial landscape.

Bogle's most significant achievement was the creation of the Vanguard 500 Index Fund in 1976, which allowed investors to own a diversified portfolio of stocks that tracked the performance of the S&P 500 at minimal cost. This innovation democratized investing, making it accessible to the average person and challenging the traditional emphasis on actively managed funds. His relentless advocacy for low fees and transparency has saved investors billions over the decades.

Beyond founding Vanguard, Bogle authored several influential books, including *Common Sense on Mutual Funds*, in which he articulated his long-term, low-cost investing philosophy. His straightforward approach emphasized patience and discipline, empowering investors to achieve financial security. Bogle's legacy endures as a champion of the individual investor, profoundly influencing how people invest for retirement and long-term goals.

*Book Title

The stock market is a giant distraction to the business of investing.
—*The Little Book of Common Sense Investing, 2007*

Don't look for the needle in the haystack. Just buy the haystack!
—*The Little Book of Common Sense Investing, 2007*

In investing, you get what you don't pay for.
—*Common Sense on Mutual Funds, 1999*

The miracle of compounding returns is overwhelmed by the tyranny of compounding costs.
—*Common Sense on Mutual Funds, 1999*

The courage to press on regardless—regardless of whether we face calm seas or rough seas, and especially when the market storms howl around us—is the quintessential attribute of the successful investor.
—*The Clash of the Cultures, 2012*

Stay the course. No matter what happens, stick to your program. I've said "Stay the course" a thousand times, and I meant it every time. It is the most important single piece of investment wisdom I can give to you.
—*The Little Book of Common Sense Investing, 2007*

The enemy of a good plan is the dream of a perfect plan.
—Bloomberg, 2013

The most important single factor in shaping our lives is the process of choosing.
—*Enough, 2008*

— JACK BOGLE

Jack Ma

(Founder of Alibaba Group)

Jack Ma (born 1964) is a Chinese entrepreneur who rose from humble beginnings to become one of the world's most influential business figures. Growing up in Hangzhou, Ma was fascinated by English and self-taught the language by offering free tours to foreign visitors. Despite facing repeated rejections, including being denied college admission twice and failing to secure numerous jobs, he persevered with an unyielding belief in the internet's transformative power.

In 1999, Ma founded Alibaba Group from his apartment to empower small businesses through e-commerce. What started as a modest online marketplace rapidly expanded into a global powerhouse, encompassing platforms like Taobao, which became China's largest online shopping destination. Alibaba's success culminated in a record-breaking IPO in 2014, solidifying Ma's reputation as a visionary leader who reshaped the landscape of digital commerce.

After stepping down as Alibaba's executive chairman in 2019, Ma focused on philanthropy, particularly education and environmental conservation. Through the Jack Ma Foundation, he has dedicated resources to improving rural education in China and supporting young entrepreneurs. Ma's journey, marked by resilience and innovation, inspires those who face challenges in pursuit of their dreams.

Never give up. Today is hard, tomorrow will be worse, but the day after tomorrow will be sunshine.
—*World Economic Forum, 2016*

Opportunities lie in the place where the complaints are.
—*CNBC, 2014*

Forget about your competitors, just focus on your customers.
—*Alibaba IPO Roadshow, 2014*

You should learn from your competitor, but never copy. Copy and you die.
—*The Financial Times, 2006*

If we are a good team and know what we want to do, one of us can defeat ten of them.
—*Bloomberg, 2014*

When you are small, you have to be very focused and rely on your brain, not your strength.
—*Business Insider, 2015*

Your attitude is more important than your capabilities. Similarly, your decision is more important than your capabilities.
—*World Economic Forum, 2015*

The greatest failure is giving up.
—*Forbes, 2013*

Before you're 30, work for a small company, learn passion, learn to dream. After you're 30, work for yourself.
—*World Economic Forum, 2015*

— JACK MA

Jamie Dimon

(CEO of JPMorgan Chase)

Jamie Dimon (born 1956) is an American business executive best known for being the CEO and Chairman of JPMorgan Chase, one of the world's largest and most influential financial institutions. Born and raised in New York City, Dimon graduated from Tufts University and later earned his MBA from Harvard Business School, where he excelled academically.

Dimon's career took off in the 1980s when he joined forces with Sandy Weill at American Express and later helped build Citigroup. In 2004, Dimon became CEO of Bank One, which merged with JPMorgan Chase shortly after, positioning him to take over as the combined company's CEO in 2005. Under his leadership, JPMorgan navigated the 2008 financial crisis with relative strength, emerging as one of the few major banks not needing a government bailout.

Dimon is widely respected for his strong management style, approach to risk management, and ability to steer JPMorgan through volatile financial markets. His tenure has been marked by consistent growth, solidifying JPMorgan Chase's position as a leading global bank while shaping key industry trends in finance and banking innovation.

The most important thing we can do is to build a company that is highly respected for its discipline, its integrity, and its professionalism.
—*Fortune, 2014*

Companies that are good to their employees, good to their customers, and good to the communities they serve tend to do better in the long run.
—*Business Insider, 2017*

In business, you're never really sure what's going to happen next. So, be prepared for the unexpected.
—*The New York Times, 2016*

I've never seen a company fail from having too much capital or too much liquidity, but I've seen many fail from having too little.
—*Bloomberg, 2013*

The key to business success is resilience – being able to keep going when times are tough, and not losing sight of your goals.
—*Fortune, 2016*

In a crisis, leadership and communication are paramount. It's about rallying the team and keeping people focused on what's important.
—*CNBC, 2020*

Tough times don't last, tough people do. But it's also important to learn from those tough times and make your business stronger for the future.
—*Fortune, 2015*

— JAMIE DIMON

Jane Fraser

(CEO of Citigroup)

Jane Fraser (born 1967) is a pioneering Scottish-American banker who made history as the first woman to lead a major Wall Street bank. Educated at Cambridge University and Harvard Business School, Fraser began her career at Goldman Sachs and McKinsey & Company, gaining extensive strategy and consulting experience.

In 2004, she joined Citigroup, where her leadership skills quickly propelled her into senior roles. She led the bank's Latin America division through economic challenges, focusing on restructuring operations and streamlining growth strategies. Fraser was instrumental in revamping Citi's global mortgage business post-2008 financial crisis and was later appointed President of Citigroup and CEO of Global Consumer Banking in 2019.

In 2021, she became CEO of Citigroup, overseeing the global bank's operations across 100 countries. Known for her pragmatic approach to leadership and focus on ethical banking practices, Fraser is widely regarded for steering Citigroup through complex regulatory environments and modernizing its operations. Her achievements mark a significant milestone in the finance industry, reflecting her commitment to innovation and inclusive leadership.

The best leaders are the ones who listen the most.
—*Harvard Business Review*, 2019

Businesses need to focus on both profit and purpose to be truly successful.
—*Citigroup's Annual Letter to Shareholders*, 2021

Success is a journey of learning, failing, and getting back up stronger each time.
—*CNBC*, 2021

It's not just about getting a seat at the table, but about making that seat count.
—*Fortune Most Powerful Women Summit*, 2020

You don't have to be the loudest person in the room to lead effectively.
—*The Financial Times*, 2020

Inclusion is key to innovation—diverse perspectives lead to better decisions.
—*Bloomberg*, 2021

You need a strong moral compass to navigate the challenges of business.
—*Citigroup Annual Report*, 2019

Empathy is one of the most powerful leadership tools—never underestimate its impact.
—*Fortune Most Powerful Women Summit*, 2020

— JANE FRASER

Jeff Bezos

(Founder and former CEO of Amazon)

Jeff Bezos (born 1964) is an American entrepreneur and founder of Amazon, one of the world's largest e-commerce companies. Born in Albuquerque, New Mexico, and raised in Houston and Miami, Bezos showed an early interest in science and technology. After graduating from Princeton University in 1986 with a degree in computer science and electrical engineering, he worked on Wall Street before recognizing the potential of the internet.

In 1994, Bezos founded Amazon in his garage in Seattle as an online bookstore. His vision quickly expanded, and Amazon became a global marketplace, revolutionizing how people shop. Under his leadership, Amazon diversified into various sectors, including cloud computing with Amazon Web Services (AWS), entertainment with Amazon Prime, and even artificial intelligence. Bezos' customer-centric approach and emphasis on innovation were crucial factors in Amazon's massive growth.

In 2021, Bezos stepped down as CEO of Amazon to focus on other ventures, including his space exploration company, Blue Origin, which aims to make space travel accessible. Bezos has also engaged in significant philanthropic efforts to combat climate change, including the Bezos Earth Fund. His contributions to e-commerce, technology, and space exploration have made him one of the most influential figures of his generation.

Your brand is what other people say about you when you're not in the room.
—*Speech at the Entrepreneurs Organization's University, 2012*

We're stubborn on vision. We're flexible on details.
—*Amazon's Annual Shareholder Letter, 2011*

If you double the number of experiments you do per year, you're going to double your inventiveness.
—*Fast Company, 2004*

If you decide that you're going to do only the things you know are going to work, you're going to leave a lot of opportunity on the table.
—*Amazon's Annual Shareholder Letter, 2015*

I think frugality drives innovation, just like other constraints do. One of the only ways to get out of a tight box is to invent your way out.
—*Business Insider, 2013*

The best customer service is if the customer doesn't need to call you, doesn't need to talk to you. It just works.
—*Amazon's Annual Shareholder Letter, 2013*

In the end, we are our choices. Build yourself a great story.
—*Princeton University Commencement Address, 2010*

Obsess about customers, not competitors.
—*Business Insider, 2012*

Work hard, have fun, make history.
—*Amazon's company slogan, 1997*

— JEFF BEZOS

Jensen Huang

(Co-founder and CEO of NVIDIA)

Jensen Huang (born 1963) is a Taiwanese-American entrepreneur and the co-founder of NVIDIA, a pioneering graphics processing and AI technology company. Born in Tainan, Taiwan, Huang moved to the U.S. as a child and later earned a degree in electrical engineering from Stanford University. In 1993, he co-founded NVIDIA, recognizing the potential of graphics processing units (GPUs) to revolutionize computing beyond gaming.

Under Huang's leadership, NVIDIA transformed from a niche graphics chipmaker into a global AI, gaming, and high-performance computing leader. The company's GPU architecture proved essential in powering advancements in artificial intelligence, deep learning, and autonomous vehicles. NVIDIA's products became vital in industries ranging from healthcare to automotive, with their GPUs used for data centers and AI training models.

Huang's forward-thinking vision and relentless drive for innovation helped NVIDIA become a major force in the tech industry. His leadership has been praised for its focus on long-term strategy, adaptability, and fostering a culture of innovation. Today, Huang is widely recognized as one of the most influential figures in technology, with NVIDIA continuing to push the boundaries of what is possible in computing and artificial intelligence.

Great companies are built by great people.
—*CNBC, 2018*

Innovation starts with seeing things differently, and that's where the magic happens.
—*Fortune, 2017*

The future is not a continuation of the past, and you can't just follow what worked yesterday.
—*Bloomberg, 2021*

Do what others think is impossible. That's how you create breakthroughs.
—*VentureBeat, 2019*

Adapt, or you're going to be left behind.
—*The Financial Times, 2019*

Speed is everything in business. The faster you iterate, the faster you succeed.
—*Harvard Business Review, 2020*

Our work is about taking risks to change the world, not just playing it safe.
—*Forbes, 2018*

The ability to see the future ahead of others is what gives you an edge in business.
—*The Economist, 2020*

Failure is part of the process. If you're not failing, you're not learning.
—*Fortune, 2019*

— JENSEN HUANG

Larry Fink

(CEO of BlackRock)

Larry Fink (born 1952) is the co-founder and CEO of BlackRock, the world's largest asset management firm. Fink began his career in the 1970s at First Boston, where he was an early pioneer in mortgage-backed securities. After a significant misstep that cost the firm millions, Fink learned the importance of risk management, a lesson that would shape his future career.

In 1988, Fink co-founded BlackRock, initially a small bond investment firm. Under his leadership, BlackRock grew exponentially, becoming a global financial powerhouse with trillions of dollars in assets under management. Fink's focus on using technology and data-driven insights transformed BlackRock into a leader in investment and risk management services.

Fink is known for his annual letters to CEOs, where he emphasizes the importance of long-term value creation, corporate responsibility, and environmental sustainability. His influence extends beyond finance, as BlackRock's decisions shape the global economy. He has become a prominent voice advocating for sustainable investing and the integration of environmental, social, and governance (ESG) criteria into business strategies.

Purpose is not the sole pursuit of profits but the animating force for achieving them.
—*Letter to CEOs, 2022*

Companies that fulfill their purpose and responsibilities to stakeholders reap rewards over the long term.
—*Letter to CEOs, 2019*

Capitalism has the power to shape society and act as a powerful agent for change.
—*Letter to CEOs, 2019*

In today's interconnected world, a company must embrace a purpose to be successful over time.
—*Letter to CEOs, 2018*

You need to be willing to evolve with the world around you, or you risk being left behind.
—*CNBC, 2020*

Business leaders cannot ignore the impact of their actions on society and the environment.
—*The Guardian, 2019*

In the future, companies that don't address sustainability will be seen as having failed their stakeholders.
—*Letter to CEOs, 2020*

Leaders must have the courage to shape the future with bold decisions and a long-term vision.
—*Bloomberg, 2019*

— LARRY FINK

Larry Page

(Co-founder and former CEO of Google)

Larry Page (born 1973) is an American computer scientist and entrepreneur who co-founded Google, one of the most influential companies in the world. Raised in East Lansing, Michigan, Page was drawn to technology from a young age, influenced by his parents, who were computer science professors. He went on to study at Stanford University, where he met Sergey Brin. Together, they developed a search engine that ranked web pages based on their relevance, which became Google in 1998.

Google revolutionized how information is accessed online, quickly becoming the dominant search engine worldwide. Under Page's leadership as CEO, Google expanded its services, launching products like Google Maps, Gmail, and Android. In 2015, he restructured Google into Alphabet Inc., a holding company, to better manage its growing array of projects, including artificial intelligence, self-driving cars, and life sciences.

Page's innovative vision and focus on long-term goals have been instrumental in Google's growth from a startup into a global tech giant. His work has transformed internet search and paved the way for advancements in technology and artificial intelligence, making him one of the most significant figures in the digital era.

Always deliver more than expected.
—*The Economist, 2002*

If you're changing the world, you're working on important things. You're excited to get up in the morning.
—*Wired, 2013*

You never lose a dream; it just incubates as a hobby.
—*Commencement speech at the University of Michigan, 2009*

It's very hard to fail completely if you aim high enough.
—*Business Insider, 2014*

You don't need to have a 100-person company to develop that idea.
—*Business Insider, 2012*

Have a healthy disregard for the impossible.
—*Stanford University commencement address, 2002*

Anything you can imagine probably is doable, you just have to imagine it and work on it.
—*The Guardian, 2013*

I think it is often easier to make progress on mega-ambitious dreams. I know that sounds completely nuts. But since no one else is crazy enough to do it, you have little competition.
—*Google I/O Developer Conference, 2013*

You can be serious without a suit.
—*Google's company culture motto, 2004*

— LARRY PAGE

Lisa Su

(CEO of AMD)

Lisa Su (born 1969) is a Taiwanese-American engineer and business executive known for transforming Advanced Micro Devices (AMD) into a global semiconductor leader. Su earned her bachelor's, master's, and PhD in electrical engineering from MIT, where she focused on semiconductor research, laying the foundation for her future in the tech industry.

Su's career began at Texas Instruments and IBM, where she contributed to semiconductor technology and microprocessor innovation. In 2012, she joined AMD, and by 2014 she was named CEO. Under her leadership, AMD launched its groundbreaking Ryzen processors and EPYC server chips, regaining market share and competitiveness against Intel and NVIDIA. Her strategic focus on high-performance computing and gaming helped revive AMD's fortunes.

Recognized as one of the most powerful women in technology, Lisa Su's leadership at AMD has been credited with driving innovation in industries ranging from gaming to data centers. She continues to play a pivotal role in advancing chip technology, positioning AMD at the forefront of the global tech industry. Her leadership style is marked by her technical expertise and a compelling vision for future growth in an ever-evolving market, inspiring those around her.

You have to not only think big, but be willing to fail big.
—*Fortune, 2021*

The key to success is being focused and having a sense of urgency about what you are trying to achieve.
—*Harvard Business Review, 2018*

You need to set audacious goals and inspire people to exceed their own expectations.
—*MIT Tech Review Innovators Under 35, 2020*

Innovation and perseverance go hand in hand.
—*CNBC, 2019*

The most important thing in leadership is making the right decision, not the easy one.
—*Fortune Most Powerful Women Summit, 2019*

You have to embrace challenges and see them as opportunities for growth.
—*MIT Technology Review, 2019*

The best way to drive progress is through constant learning and adaptation.
—*CNBC, 2020*

Great companies are built on great products, but also on the ability to reinvent and redefine themselves over time.
—*Fortune, 2018*

You have to believe in what you're doing and communicate that passion to your team.
—*Harvard Business Review, 2019*

— LISA SU

Marc Benioff

(Founder and CEO of Salesforce)

Marc Benioff (born 1964) is an American entrepreneur and philanthropist best known as the co-founder and CEO of Salesforce, a leading cloud computing company. After graduating from the University of Southern California, Benioff started his career at Oracle Corporation, where he quickly rose through the ranks. By age 26, he was a vice president, but his entrepreneurial spirit led him to leave Oracle and pursue a new vision.

In 1999, Benioff co-founded Salesforce to revolutionize software delivery by moving it to the cloud. Under his leadership, Salesforce grew from a startup into a global powerhouse, reshaping the enterprise software industry and pioneering the Software-as-a-Service (SaaS) model. The company's flagship product, a customer relationship management (CRM) platform, has become integral to businesses worldwide, and Salesforce is consistently recognized as one of the most innovative companies globally.

Beyond his business achievements, Benioff is known for his commitment to social responsibility. He championed Salesforce's 1-1-1 philanthropic model, dedicating 1% of the company's equity, product, and employees' time to charitable causes. He also advocates for social issues, such as equality in the workplace and homelessness, using his platform to influence corporate and public policy.

*Book Title

The business of business is improving the state of the world.
—*Speech at Dreamforce Conference, 2006*

You must always be able to predict what's next and then have the flexibility to evolve.
—*Forbes, 2014*

To be truly successful, companies need to have a corporate mission that is bigger than making a profit.
—*Harvard Business Review, 2013*

The secret to successful hiring is this: look for the people who want to change the world.
—**Behind the Cloud, 2009*

Speed is the new currency of business.
—*CNBC, 2017*

Innovation comes from people meeting up in the hallways or calling each other at 10:30 at night with a new idea.
—*The New York Times, 2012*

The real competitive advantage in any business is one word only, which is "people".
—*Speech at World Economic Forum, 2011*

We need to integrate philanthropy into businesses in a way that will truly make a difference.
—**Trailblazer, 2019*

It's not just about technology and innovation. It's about helping people and creating meaningful impact in the world.
—*Harvard Business Review, 2019*

— MARC BENIOFF

Marillyn Hewson

(Former CEO of Lockheed Martin)

Marillyn Hewson (born 1953) is an American business leader best known for her tenure as CEO and Chair of Lockheed Martin, one of the largest defense contractors in the world. Hewson earned her bachelor's degree in business administration and later an MBA from the University of Alabama. She joined Lockheed Martin in 1983 and held a variety of roles in the company before becoming CEO in 2013.

During her leadership, Hewson transformed Lockheed Martin's operations by securing major defense contracts, including the F-35 fighter jet program. Under her guidance, the company expanded its technological focus in areas like cybersecurity, space exploration, and missile defense. By the time she stepped down in 2020, Lockheed Martin's revenue had grown substantially, and the company became a critical player in the defense and innovation sectors.

Hewson has consistently been recognized as one of the most powerful women in business, appearing on lists like Fortune's "Most Powerful Women". Her leadership at Lockheed Martin left a lasting impact on the aerospace and defense industries, cementing her legacy as a key figure in corporate America.

The most important thing you can do as a leader is to inspire your team to see the vision and then give them the tools to achieve it.
—*Harvard Business Review, 2018*

Empowerment means giving your team the authority and responsibility to succeed on their own terms.
—*The Wall Street Journal, 2019*

Your greatest asset as a leader is the trust of your employees. Without that, nothing else works.
—*CNBC, 2017*

A culture of integrity is non-negotiable if you want to build a sustainable, successful business.
—*Lockheed Martin Annual Report, 2019*

It's not enough to manage the present; you must also prepare for the future.
—*Fortune Most Powerful Women Summit, 2018*

Great leaders know how to align the right people with the right tasks, at the right time.
—*Forbes, 2018*

Leadership is about setting the right example, fostering collaboration, and inspiring excellence.
—*MIT Sloan Management Review, 2017*

Innovation is not just about technology; it's about creating an environment where people feel empowered to think big and take risks.
—*Fortune Most Powerful Women Summit, 2018*

— MARILLYN HEWSON

Marissa Mayer

(Former CEO of Yahoo)

Marissa Mayer (born 1975) is a trailblazing figure in the tech industry, known for her influential roles at both Google and Yahoo. Raised in Wausau, Wisconsin, Mayer showed early promise in mathematics and science, which led her to Stanford University, where she earned degrees in symbolic systems and computer science. In 1999, she joined Google as its 20th employee and first female engineer, contributing to the design and user experience of some of its most iconic products, including Google Search and Gmail.

In 2012, Mayer took on the challenge of leading Yahoo as its CEO. Her tenure was marked by efforts to revitalize the struggling internet giant, including the acquisition of Tumblr and a focus on mobile technology. Although Yahoo's long-term turnaround proved elusive, Mayer's leadership kept the company in the spotlight and highlighted the importance of user-centric design in tech innovation.

After stepping down from Yahoo following its acquisition by Verizon in 2017, Mayer co-founded Lumi Labs, which focuses on building consumer applications powered by artificial intelligence. Mayer's career is a testament to her resilience and pioneering spirit in a male-dominated industry, where she has consistently pushed the boundaries of what technology can achieve.

I always did something I was a little not ready to do. I think that's how you grow.
—*Vogue*, 2013

You can't have everything you want, but you can have the things that really matter to you.
—*Commencement speech at Illinois Institute of Technology*, 2009

I think the most successful people work smart, not hard.
—*CNN*, 2014

When you need to innovate, you need collaboration.
—*World Economic Forum*, 2013

The difference between successful people and others is how long they spend time feeling sorry for themselves.
—*Business Insider*, 2013

I refuse to be slowed down by perfectionism when it prevents me from being productive.
—*The New York Times*, 2013

Creativity loves constraints.
—*VentureBeat*, 2009

It's important to be willing to make mistakes. The worst thing that can happen is you become memorable.
—*Business Insider*, 2013

People ask me why I do things that are risky, and the truth is, every time I do something I fear, I gain more confidence.
—*Glamour*, 2012

— MARISSA MAYER

Mark Zuckerberg

(Co-founder and CEO of Facebook)

Mark Zuckerberg (born 1984) is an American entrepreneur best known as the co-founder and CEO of Facebook, the world's largest social media platform. Zuckerberg was raised in Dobbs Ferry, New York, where he developed an early interest in computers and programming. He attended Harvard University, where he launched "The Facebook" in 2004 from his dorm room, initially as a social networking site for college students.

Under Zuckerberg's leadership, Facebook quickly expanded beyond universities, becoming a global phenomenon that revolutionized how people connect and share information online. His vision and leadership led to the acquisition of companies like Instagram and WhatsApp. In 2021, it was rebranded as Meta to reflect a broader focus on virtual and augmented reality, including the metaverse development.

Zuckerberg has faced challenges, including scrutiny over privacy practices and the platform's role in disseminating information. Despite these issues, he remains a central figure in the tech industry, steering Meta toward new frontiers in digital communication and virtual spaces. His impact on how people interact online has made him one of the most influential figures in the digital age.

Move fast and break things. Unless you are breaking stuff, you are not moving fast enough.
—*Business Insider, 2009*

In a world that's changing really quickly, the only strategy that is guaranteed to fail is not taking risks.
—*Y Combinator's Startup School, 2011*

Building a mission and building a business go hand in hand.
—*Fortune, 2012*

The question I ask myself like almost every day is, "Am I doing the most important thing I could be doing?"
—*The New Yorker, 2010*

Find that thing you are super passionate about.
—*Commencement Address at Harvard University, 2017*

Ideas don't come out fully formed. They only become clear as you work on them. You just have to get started.
—*Commencement Address at Harvard University, 2017*

People can be really smart or have skills that are directly applicable, but if they don't really believe in it, then they are not going to really work hard.
—*Business Insider, 2010*

If you just work on stuff that you like and you're passionate about, you don't have to have a master plan with how things will play out.
—*TechCrunch Disrupt, 2012*

— MARK ZUCKERBERG

Mary Barra

(CEO of General Motors)

Mary Barra (born 1961) is an American business executive known for being the first female CEO of General Motors (GM), a position she assumed in 2014. Her career at GM began in 1980 as a co-op student, balancing her studies at General Motors Institute (now Kettering University) with practical work experience. Over the decades, Barra rose through the ranks, holding various positions in engineering and management, which solidified her expertise and reputation within the company.

As CEO, Barra has led GM through significant transformations, including the company's pivot towards electric vehicles and autonomous driving technology. Under her leadership, GM committed to an all-electric future, announcing plans to phase out gasoline and diesel-powered cars. She also navigated the company through challenging times, including the 2014 ignition switch recall crisis, demonstrating her focus on accountability and safety.

Barra's leadership extends beyond GM. She has been a powerful advocate for diversity and inclusion in the automotive industry. She serves on the board of directors for several major organizations and has been recognized globally for her influence and impact, including being listed among the world's most powerful women by *Forbes*. Her tenure as CEO marks a new era for GM, steering the company towards a sustainable and innovative future.

If you do every job like you're going to do it for the rest of your life, that's when you get noticed.
—*Fortune, 2013*

You've got to run your own race. Everybody has a different path, and what's important is that you follow it and have the courage to pursue your passion.
—*Speech at Stanford Graduate School of Business, 2015*

My definition of "innovative" is providing value to the customer.
—*Harvard Business Review, 2014*

The way to succeed is to double down on what's working, and just keep working harder and smarter.
—*Fortune, 2015*

I believe the customer is going to be our compass. It's the customer that will lead us where we need to go.
—*CBS This Morning, 2014*

When you have a winning culture, people are excited to come to work.
—*Fortune's Most Powerful Women Summit, 2015*

We have to get comfortable with the discomfort of going through change.
—*Business Insider, 2017*

Sometimes you have to take the harder path.
—*The New York Times, 2014*

— MARY BARRA

Meg Whitman

(Former CEO of HP and eBay)

Meg Whitman (born 1956) is a highly respected business executive known for leadership in several major companies. After earning degrees from Princeton University and Harvard Business School, Whitman began her career at Procter & Gamble and later held executive positions at companies like Disney and Hasbro. Her most notable achievement came when she became the CEO of eBay in 1998. At the time, eBay was a small startup, but under Whitman's leadership, it grew into a global e-commerce giant with millions of users.

After leaving eBay in 2008, Whitman served as CEO of Hewlett-Packard (HP), where she led a significant restructuring that resulted in the company splitting into two separate entities, HP Inc. and Hewlett Packard Enterprise. This move was part of a broader strategy to better focus on the differing demands of technology and services markets. Her focus on efficiency and innovation marked Whitman's leadership at HP during a challenging time for the tech industry.

In addition to her corporate achievements, Whitman made a bid for political office in 2010, running as the Republican candidate for Governor of California. Though she did not win, her business and public service career have made her a prominent figure in American business and beyond.

Book Title

The price of inaction is far greater than the cost of a mistake.
—*Harvard Business Review*, 2005

When people use your brand name as a verb, that is remarkable.
—*The Power of Many*, 2010

You can always find a solution if you try hard enough.
—*Business Insider*, 2011

Run to the fire; don't hide from it.
—*Commencement speech at Princeton University*, 2005

Do what you love and success will follow. Passion is the fuel behind a successful career.
—*The Power of Many*, 2010

One of the secret benefits of using remote workers is that the work itself becomes the yardstick to judge someone's performance.
—*Fortune*, 2012

I have a pretty simple rule: work hard, be honest, and when you see a problem, fix it.
—*Commencement speech at Whitman College*, 2012

The ability to communicate your idea clearly and effectively is critical.
—*Fast Company*, 2010

You have to have confidence in your vision or you will be knocked down by those who criticize it.
—*Forbes*, 2015

— MEG WHITMAN

Melanie Perkins

(Co-founder and CEO of Canva)

Melanie Perkins (born 1987) is an Australian entrepreneur and co-founder of Canva, a graphic design platform that revolutionized how people create digital content. Raised in Perth, Perkins began her entrepreneurial journey while still in university, where she taught design programs to fellow students and noticed how complex and inaccessible traditional design software was.

In 2012, Perkins and co-founder Cliff Obrecht launched Canva to simplify the design process. Initially focused on the yearbook market, Canva soon expanded into a global platform offering easy-to-use design tools for everything from social media graphics to business presentations. Today, Canva serves millions of users worldwide and is valued as one of Australia's most successful tech companies.

Perkins has been recognized for her visionary leadership and perseverance. In the early stages of Canva, she overcame numerous rejections from investors before securing funding and turning it into a multi-billion-dollar enterprise. Her impact on democratizing design has made her a prominent figure in tech and entrepreneurship, and she continues to drive innovation in the digital content space.

If you're determined enough and willing to work hard enough, you can make just about anything happen.
—*The New York Times*, 2020

The biggest thing you can do to drive innovation is have a diverse team.
—*Forbes*, 2021

One of the best things about starting a company is you get to craft the culture that you wish you'd worked in.
—*The Guardian*, 2019

Solve a real problem that real people are having and solve it in a simple and fun way.
—*Inc.*, 2020

We always strive to make complex things simple.
—*Business Insider Australia*, 2020

You have to be insanely passionate about what you're doing because building a company is incredibly hard work.
—*The New York Times*, 2020

As a leader, you have to stay true to your vision and keep that at the forefront of every decision you make.
—*Forbes*, 2021

A clear mission helps attract the right people and keeps everyone aligned.
—*Inc.*, 2020

Start before you're ready. Don't prepare, just begin.
—*Inc.*, 2019

— MELANIE PERKINS

Michael Bloomberg

(Founder and former CEO of Bloomberg LP)

Michael Bloomberg (born 1942) is an American entrepreneur, philanthropist, and politician widely recognized as the co-founder of Bloomberg L.P., a global financial information and media company. After earning an MBA from Harvard Business School in 1966, Bloomberg began his career at Salomon Brothers, an investment bank, where he quickly ascended to partner. However, he was laid off in 1981, a setback that led him to launch his own company.

In 1981, Bloomberg used his severance to start Innovative Market Systems, which would later become Bloomberg L.P. The company revolutionized how financial data was delivered, providing real-time market data and analytics through its Bloomberg Terminal. This innovation became an essential tool for financial professionals, propelling the company to global prominence.

Bloomberg's influence extends beyond business. He served three terms as the Mayor of New York City from 2002 to 2013, where he implemented policies to improve public health, education, and environmental sustainability. As a philanthropist, Bloomberg has donated billions to causes, including public health, education, and climate change, through his foundation, Bloomberg Philanthropies. His approach to business and governance reflects a commitment to data-driven decision-making and public service.

I've always respected those who tried to change the world for the better, rather than just complain about it.
—*Commencement speech at Tufts University, 2014*

In business, you have to be willing to take risks. The biggest risk is not taking any risks.
—*Harvard Business Review, 2012*

The hardest thing to do is to start. You have to take that first step, and the rest will follow.
—*Fast Company, 2009*

If you're going to succeed, you need a vision, the self-confidence to believe you can get there, and the leadership skills to bring people with you.
—*Speech at Johns Hopkins University, 2013*

Being an entrepreneur isn't really about starting a business. It's a way of looking at the world: seeing opportunity where others see obstacles, taking risks when others take refuge.
—*Business Insider, 2013*

Progress and innovation happen when you set ambitious goals and find ways to reach them.
—*The New York Times, 2013*

Don't be afraid to assert yourself, have confidence in your abilities and don't let the bastards get you down.
—*Fortune, 2013*

You have to take risks. We will only understand the miracle of life fully when we allow the unexpected to happen.
—*Forbes, 2014*

— MICHAEL BLOOMBERG

Michael Dell

(Founder and CEO of Dell Technologies)

Michael Dell (born 1965) is a pioneering entrepreneur and the founder of Dell Technologies, one of the world's largest technology companies. Dell's entrepreneurial journey began as a student at the University of Texas at Austin, where he started selling custom-built computers directly to customers. Recognizing the potential of bypassing traditional retail channels, Dell dropped out of college in 1984 to focus on his business, founding Dell Computer Corporation. His direct-to-consumer model revolutionized the personal computer industry, allowing the company to grow rapidly.

Under Dell's leadership, the company expanded its product offerings beyond PCs to servers, storage, and networking equipment, eventually becoming a global technology leader. In 2013, Dell took the company private in one of the largest leveraged buyouts in history, allowing him greater flexibility to steer the company's long-term strategy. In 2016, Dell orchestrated the acquisition of EMC Corporation, a significant player in cloud computing and data storage, further transforming Dell Technologies into a comprehensive provider of IT solutions.

Dell's business philosophy emphasizes customer feedback and direct relationships, which have been critical to his company's success. Beyond his business ventures, Michael Dell is also known for his philanthropic efforts, mainly through the Michael & Susan Dell Foundation, which focuses on education, health, and family economic stability.

Book Title

Recognize that there will be failures, and acknowledge that there will be obstacles. But you will learn from your mistakes and the mistakes of others, for there is very little learning in success.
—*Entrepreneur, 1998*

Ideas are a commodity. Execution of them is not.
—*Forbes, 1996*

You don't have to be a genius or a visionary or even a college graduate to be successful. You just need a framework and a dream.
—**Direct from Dell, 1999*

Try never to be the smartest person in the room. And if you are, I suggest you invite smarter people... or find a different room.
—*Success Magazine, 2013*

Whether you are a startup or a large company, innovation is the only way to win in the market.
—*Forbes, 2012*

The key to winning is to operate in a totally transparent way.
—*Fortune, 2015*

Technology is about enabling human potential.
—*Fast Company, 2010*

If you have to be someone, be the one that gets to make the decisions.
—*Harvard Business Review, 2004*

— MICHAEL DELL

Oprah Winfrey

(Founder of OWN Network)

Oprah Winfrey (born 1954) rose from humble beginnings in rural Mississippi to become one of the most influential media moguls in the world. Her career took off in the 1980s when she became the host of *The Oprah Winfrey Show*, which ran for 25 years and became the highest-rated talk show in television history. Known for her empathetic interviewing style and ability to connect with audiences, Winfrey transformed her show into a platform for tackling various topics, from personal development to social issues.

Beyond television, Winfrey has made a significant impact as a producer, actress, and philanthropist. She founded Harpo Productions, through which she produced films like *The Color Purple* and *Selma*. In 2011, she launched the Oprah Winfrey Network (OWN), further expanding her influence in the media industry. Her book club started in 1996 and became a literary force, turning many titles into bestsellers and fostering a renewed interest in reading.

Winfrey's influence extends far beyond the media. She is a dedicated philanthropist who has made significant contributions to education and empowerment initiatives, including the establishment of the Oprah Winfrey Leadership Academy for Girls in South Africa. Her legacy is one of resilience, innovation, and a commitment to using her platform for positive change.

The biggest adventure you can take is to live the life of your dreams.
—*O, The Oprah Magazine, 2005*

You know you are on the road to success if you would do your job and not be paid for it.
—*Commencement speech at Stanford University, 2008*

I don't believe in failure. It is not failure if you enjoyed the process.
—*The Oprah Winfrey Show, 1994*

The key to realizing a dream is to focus not on success, but on significance—and then even the small steps and little victories along your path will take on greater meaning.
—*O, The Oprah Magazine, 2002*

Surround yourself only with people who are going to lift you higher.
—*O, The Oprah Magazine, 1997*

Challenges are gifts that force us to search for a new center of gravity. Don't fight them. Just find a new way to stand.
—*O, The Oprah Magazine, 2010*

Passion is energy. Feel the power that comes from focusing on what excites you.
—*O, The Oprah Magazine, 2002*

You don't become what you want, you become what you believe.
—*O, The Oprah Magazine, 2002*

— OPRAH WINFREY

Phil Knight

(Co-founder and former CEO of Nike, Inc.)

Phil Knight (born 1938) co-founded Nike, Inc., a global athletic footwear and apparel leader. His journey began in 1964 when he started the company as Blue Ribbon Sports, selling Japanese running shoes out of the trunk of his car. Knight's partnership with Bill Bowerman, his former track coach at the University of Oregon, laid the foundation for what would become one of the most recognizable brands in the world.

Under Knight's leadership, Nike revolutionized the sports industry with innovative products and groundbreaking marketing strategies. The introduction of the "Just Do It" campaign and endorsements from athletes like Michael Jordan helped cement Nike's status as a cultural icon. By the time Knight stepped down as CEO in 2004, Nike had grown into a multi-billion-dollar corporation with a global presence.

In addition to his business success, Knight has made significant contributions to education and philanthropy. He has donated hundreds of millions to institutions such as the University of Oregon and Stanford University. Knight's legacy is not only defined by the global empire he built but also by his impact on sports, culture, and philanthropy, making him one of the most influential figures in modern business history.

Book Title

Play by the rules, but be ferocious.
—*Shoe Dog, 2016*

The only time you must not fail is the last time you try.
—*Shoe Dog, 2016*

There is no finish line.
—*Nike Advertisement, 1977*

Entrepreneurs have to be ready for the highs and the lows, the good times and the bad, but most of all, they have to be ready to embrace uncertainty.
—*Stanford Graduate School of Business, 2009*

The cowards never started, and the weak died along the way. That leaves us, ladies and gentlemen. Us.
—*Shoe Dog, 2016*

You can't explain much in 60 seconds, but when you show Michael Jordan, you don't have to. It's that simple.
—*Sports Illustrated, 1992*

Ultimately, we wanted Nike to be the world's best sports and fitness company. Once you say that, you have a focus.
—*Harvard Business Review, 2000*

History is one long processional of crazy ideas.
—*Shoe Dog, 2016*

For a brand to be truly successful, it has to connect with the public, not just on a physical level but on an emotional level too.
—*Businessweek, 1998*

— PHIL KNIGHT

Reed Hastings

(Co-founder and Executive Chairman of Netflix)

Reed Hastings (born 1960) is a visionary entrepreneur known for transforming the entertainment industry with the founding of Netflix. After earning a degree in mathematics from Bowdoin College, Hastings served in the Peace Corps, where he taught math in Swaziland. This experience sparked his interest in education and technology, leading him to pursue a master's degree in computer science at Stanford University.

In 1997, Hastings co-founded Netflix, initially a DVD rental service that quickly became a household name. Recognizing the potential of online streaming, he led Netflix's pivot to digital content delivery in 2007, a move that revolutionized how people watch TV and movies. Under his leadership, Netflix began producing original content in 2013, starting with *House of Cards*, which significantly altered the television landscape by mainstreaming high-quality streaming content.

Hastings is also known for his commitment to education, reflecting his early experiences in Swaziland. He has been actively involved in educational reform, advocating for charter schools and serving on various academic boards. Hastings' ability to foresee and capitalize on technological trends has made him a pivotal figure in the entertainment and education sectors.

Most entrepreneurial ideas will sound crazy, stupid, and uneconomic, and then they'll turn out to be right.
—*Wired*, 2018

Do not tolerate brilliant jerks. The cost to teamwork is too high.
—*Netflix Culture Deck*, 2009

There's no better advertising than word of mouth.
—*Fortune*, 2005

I take pride in making as few decisions as possible, as many as possible by the collective.
—*Fast Company*, 2016

Don't get distracted by the shiny object [and] don't be driven by technology.
—*Wired*, 2013

Companies rarely die from moving too fast, and they frequently die from moving too slowly.
—*The New York Times*, 2018

To be a truly creative company, you must start things that might fail.
—*Wired*, 2018

I think if you're a good person and a good company, people will recognize that.
—*Business Insider*, 2016

Focusing on the future is the key to success in business.
—*Harvard Business Review*, 2018

— REED HASTINGS

Richard Branson

(Founder of Virgin Group)

Richard Branson (born 1950) is a British entrepreneur, philanthropist, and adventurer, best known as the founder of the Virgin Group. Born in London, Branson struggled with dyslexia and dropped out of school at 16, but he quickly channeled his energy into the business. He launched his first venture, a magazine called *Student*, before expanding into the music industry with Virgin Records in 1972, which became one of the world's top record labels, signing artists like the Sex Pistols and Phil Collins.

Branson's Virgin brand is a testament to his versatility and adaptability. It grew into a global conglomerate, not confined to a single industry, but spanning diverse sectors such as airlines, telecommunications, and even space travel. In 1984, he founded Virgin Atlantic, a major airline known for its customer service and innovation. Branson's adventurous spirit also led him to set several world records, including the fastest transatlantic flight in a hot air balloon. His willingness to take risks and challenge established norms has made him a prominent figure in business.

In addition to his entrepreneurial achievements, Branson is a committed philanthropist, focusing on environmental and social issues through initiatives like The Elders and Virgin Unite. His memoir, *Losing My Virginity*, offers insights into his life and business philosophy, and has inspired countless aspiring entrepreneurs worldwide.

*Book Title

Business opportunities are like buses, there's always another one coming.
—*The Times*, 2008

You don't learn to walk by following rules. You learn by doing, and by falling over.
—*Losing My Virginity*, 1998

Take a chance—it's the best way to test yourself, have fun and push boundaries.
—*Screw It, Let's Do It*, 2006

Clients do not come first. Employees come first. If you take care of your employees, they will take care of the clients.
—*The Telegraph*, 2014

A business is simply an idea to make other people's lives better.
—*Business Stripped Bare*, 2008

There is no greater thing you can do with your life and your work than follow your passions—in a way that serves the world and you.
—*The Virgin Way*, 2014

Train people well enough so they can leave, treat them well enough so they don't want to.
—*Interview with LinkedIn*, 2014

The art of delegation is one of the key skills any entrepreneur must master.
—*Like a Virgin*, 2012

— RICHARD BRANSON

Rosalind Brewer

(Former CEO of Walgreens Boots Alliance)

Rosalind Brewer (born 1962) is an influential American businesswoman who has held top leadership roles at some of the world's largest companies. Brewer earned a degree in chemistry from Spelman College before beginning her career at Kimberly-Clark. She later joined Walmart, where she rose to become CEO of Sam's Club in 2012, making her the first African-American woman to lead a Walmart division.

Brewer continued to break barriers when she joined Starbucks in 2017 as Chief Operating Officer, driving significant growth and leading initiatives focused on expanding diversity within the company. Her strategic leadership helped Starbucks innovate in retail operations and expand its global presence, particularly in digital platforms.

In 2021, Brewer became the CEO of Walgreens Boots Alliance, making her one of the few Black women leading a Fortune 500 company. At Walgreens, she has focused on expanding healthcare services, particularly in underserved communities, and driving digital transformation. Brewer's career is marked by her ability to lead major corporations through growth and transformation while championing diversity and inclusion.

Growth and comfort do not coexist.
—*CNN, 2016*

You can't change what you don't confront.
—*Forbes, 2020*

The most successful leaders are the ones who empower others.
—*Harvard Business Review, 2018*

You must never be afraid to challenge the norm and push for what is right.
—*Fortune Most Powerful Women Summit, 2017*

To lead, you have to be comfortable with being uncomfortable.
—*CNN, 2016*

Diversity is a fact, but inclusion is a choice.
—*Forbes Women's Summit, 2018*

You can't lead by following others; you have to be willing to carve your own path.
—*The Wall Street Journal, 2021*

You must know your own worth before expecting others to recognize it.
—*Inc., 2019*

True success comes from serving a purpose greater than yourself.
—*Harvard Business Review, 2018*

— ROSALIND BREWER

Sara Blakely

(Founder of Spanx)

Sara Blakely (born 1971) is an American entrepreneur best known as the founder of Spanx, a company that revolutionized the shapewear industry. Blakely started her career in sales, working for a fax machine company, but always harbored entrepreneurial ambitions. In 1998, with just $5,000 in savings, she developed the idea for footless pantyhose, which would later evolve into Spanx. Despite having no formal training in fashion, she managed to create a prototype and secure a patent.

Blakely's persistence paid off when she landed her first significant order from Neiman Marcus. Spanx quickly gained popularity, thanks in part to Blakely's grassroots marketing efforts and the support of high-profile celebrities like Oprah Winfrey. The brand expanded to include a wide range of undergarments, becoming a staple in women's wardrobes and making Blakely one of the youngest self-made female billionaires.

In addition to her success with Spanx, Blakely is known for her philanthropic efforts. She signed the Giving Pledge, committing to donate half of her wealth to charity, and has supported numerous causes, particularly those focused on empowering women. Her journey from a struggling salesperson to a global business leader is a testament to her ingenuity and determination.

Book Title

Embrace what you don't know, especially in the beginning, because what you don't know can become your greatest asset.
—*Forbes*, 2012

The biggest risk in life is not risking.
—*CNBC*, 2018

You've got to visualize where you're headed and be very clear about it.
—*Business Insider*, 2015

Ideas, even million-dollar ones, are completely worthless unless you can put them into action.
—**The Belly Art Project*, 2016

My dad encouraged us to fail. Growing up, he would ask us what we failed at that week. If we didn't have something, he'd be disappointed.
—*The Huffington Post*, 2013

Most of us want to be liked. We want to be respected. And I think that's the greatest obstacle to success.
—*CNN*, 2013

Don't be afraid to start small, because that's where you can have the most impact.
—*Business Insider*, 2015

You can have a great product, but you have to be able to tell people about it in a way that convinces them they can't live without it.
—*Inc.*, 2012

— SARA BLAKELY

Satya Nadella

(CEO of Microsoft)

Satya Nadella (born 1967) is an Indian-American business executive known for transforming Microsoft as its CEO. Born in Hyderabad, India, Nadella earned degrees in electrical engineering from Mangalore University, computer science from the University of Wisconsin-Milwaukee, and an MBA from the University of Chicago. His early career at Microsoft, which he joined in 1992, involved critical roles in the company's cloud computing, server, and tools divisions.

When Nadella took the reins as CEO of Microsoft in 2014, he brought a strategic vision that would reshape the company. Under his leadership, Microsoft significantly pivoted cloud computing, with Azure becoming a cornerstone of its business strategy. This shift, coupled with a renewed focus on artificial intelligence, productivity software, and cross-platform services, breathed new life into the company. Nadella's tenure also saw Microsoft making significant acquisitions, such as LinkedIn and GitHub, further solidifying its influence in the tech industry.

Nadella's leadership style emphasizes empathy, collaboration, and continuous learning, which has reshaped Microsoft's culture. His approach has driven financial success and reinvigorated Microsoft's innovation and relevance in a rapidly changing tech landscape. Nadella's vision has made Microsoft one of the world's most valuable companies, marking a new era of growth and adaptability.

Book Title

Be passionate and bold. Always keep learning. You stop doing useful things if you don't learn.
—*Hit Refresh, 2017*

It's not about being perfect. It's not about where you started. It's about learning and growing along the way.
—*Harvard Business Review, 2017*

You renew yourself every day. Sometimes you're successful, sometimes you're not, but it's the average that counts.
—*Hit Refresh, 2017*

Don't be a know-it-all; be a learn-it-all.
—*Interview with LinkedIn, 2016*

The notion of work-life balance is without meaning for most people. There's only life.
—*The Wall Street Journal, 2017*

The true scarce commodity of the near future will be human attention.
—*Quartz, 2016*

We must always reflect on how we can do better, because the minute we lose that curiosity, we've lost it.
—*Microsoft Annual Shareholders Meeting, 2016*

Empathy makes you a better innovator. If I look at the most successful people—whether they are design engineers, marketers, or salespeople—the best ones are the ones who can truly connect and empathize with customers.
—*Harvard Business Review, 2017*

— SATYA NADELLA

Sergey Brin

(Co-founder of Google and former President of Alphabet)

Sergey Brin (born 1973) is a computer scientist and entrepreneur best known as the co-founder of Google. Born in Moscow, Brin emigrated to the United States with his family at the age of six, seeking freedom from the Soviet Union's anti-Semitic policies. Brin's early interest in mathematics and computers led him to study computer science at Stanford University, where he met Larry Page. The duo collaborated on a research project that would become Google, the world's most popular search engine.

In 1998, Brin and Page launched Google from a garage in California, revolutionizing the way people access information. Google's innovative PageRank algorithm set it apart from other search engines, leading to its rapid growth and dominance in the tech industry. Beyond search, Brin has been instrumental in expanding Google's reach into different areas, including advertising, cloud computing, and mobile technology, through the development of products like AdWords, Google Maps, and Android.

Brin's achievements extend beyond Google, mainly through his work with Alphabet Inc., Google's parent company, where he focused on forward-thinking projects such as autonomous vehicles and life sciences. His vision and leadership have impacted the technological landscape, influencing how people interact with information and technology worldwide.

Solving big problems is easier than solving little problems.
—*Wired*, 2013

Any conversation I have about innovation starts with the ultimate goal.
—*Fast Company*, 2011

We are not going to speculate about the future. We are going to do our best to get there and shape it.
—*Businessweek*, 2003

We want to make sure that everything we do is something that, when you look back at it, you think it was a good thing to do.
—*Wired*, 2005

I feel there is an existential angst among young people. I didn't have that. They see enormous mountains, where I only saw one little hill to climb.
—*The Economist*, 2011

We will be out there doing things, making mistakes, fixing them, trying again.
—*Wired*, 2013

When it comes to creating great products, vision is overrated. It's not as important to be the first as it is to be better.
—*The Economist*, 2004

Sometimes it's important to wake up and stop dreaming. When a really great dream shows up, grab it.
—*The Economist*, 2011

— SERGEY BRIN

Sheryl Sandberg

(Founder of LeanIn.Org and former COO of Facebook)

Sheryl Sandberg (born 1969) is a prominent business executive, author, and advocate for women's leadership in the workplace. She began her career in government, serving as Chief of Staff to U.S. Treasury Secretary Larry Summers. Sandberg later transitioned into the tech industry, joining Google in 2001, where she played a pivotal role in developing the company's profitable advertising programs.

In 2008, Sandberg became the Chief Operating Officer of Facebook (now Meta), a move that significantly impacted the company's trajectory. Her leadership was instrumental in transforming the social media platform into a profitable enterprise, scaling the company's advertising business and driving significant revenue growth. Sandberg is also known for advocating gender equality and leadership, most notably through her bestselling book *Lean In: Women, Work, and the Will to Lead* (2013), which inspired a global movement encouraging women to pursue their ambitions.

Beyond her work as a writer, Sandberg is a philanthropist who focuses on issues such as education, women's rights, and poverty alleviation. She founded LeanIn.Org, a nonprofit that empowers women to achieve their goals. Sandberg's influence extends beyond business as she continues to shape conversations around leadership, gender equality, and work-life balance.

*Book Title

Leadership is about making others better as a result of your presence and making sure that impact lasts in your absence.
—TED Talk, 2010

If you're offered a seat on a rocket ship, don't ask what seat! Just get on.
—*Lean In, 2013

Done is better than perfect.
—The Guardian, 2012

We cannot change what we are not aware of, and once we are aware, we cannot help but change.
—*Lean In, 2013

Motivation comes from working on things we care about. It also comes from working with people we care about.
—*Lean In, 2013

The most important career decision you'll make is who your life partner is.
—Fortune, 2013

Feeling confident—or pretending that you feel confident—is necessary to reach for opportunities. It's a cliché, but opportunities are rarely offered; they're seized.
—*Lean In, 2013

The upside of painful knowledge is so much greater than the downside of blissful ignorance.
—Facebook post, 2016

— SHERYL SANDBERG

Steve Jobs

(Co-founder and former CEO of Apple Inc.)

Steve Jobs (1955-2011) was a visionary entrepreneur and co-founder of Apple Inc., whose innovations transformed the technology industry. Born in San Francisco, Jobs was adopted and raised in Silicon Valley, where his interest in electronics developed early. After a brief stint at Reed College, he joined forces with Steve Wozniak and Ronald Wayne in 1976 to create Apple, launching the Apple I, which revolutionized personal computing.

Under Jobs' leadership, Apple introduced groundbreaking products such as the Macintosh in 1984, the first commercially successful personal computer with a graphical user interface. However, internal conflicts led to his departure from Apple in 1985. Jobs then founded NeXT, a computer platform development company, and acquired Pixar, a small graphics company he transformed into a leading animation studio, producing hits like *Toy Story*.

In 1997, Jobs returned to Apple, rescuing it from near bankruptcy. During his tenure, he launched the iMac, iPod, iPhone, and iPad, products that not only redefined their categories but also solidified Apple's status as a global leader in innovation. Jobs' relentless pursuit of perfection and his focus on design and user experience left an indelible mark on the technology industry and modern culture.

The only way to do great work is to love what you do. If you haven't found it yet, keep looking. Don't settle.
—*Stanford University Commencement Speech, 2005*

Have the courage to follow your heart and intuition. They somehow already know what you truly want to become. Everything else is secondary.
—*Stanford University Commencement Speech, 2005*

I'm convinced that about half of what separates the successful entrepreneurs from the non-successful ones is pure perseverance.
—*Smithsonian Magazine, 1995*

Your time is limited, so don't waste it living someone else's life.
—*Stanford University Commencement Speech, 2005*

Remembering that you are going to die is the best way I know to avoid the trap of thinking you have something to lose. You are already naked. There is no reason not to follow your heart.
—*Stanford University Commencement Speech, 2005*

The people who are crazy enough to think they can change the world are the ones who do.
—*Apple's Think Different ad campaign, 1997*

My favorite things in life don't cost any money. It's really clear that the most precious resource we all have is time.
—*Interview in Playboy magazine, 1985*

Stay hungry, stay foolish.
—*Stanford University Commencement Speech, 2005*

— STEVE JOBS

Sundar Pichai

(CEO of Alphabet and Google)

Sundar Pichai (born 1972) is an Indian-American business executive known for his role as the CEO of Alphabet Inc. and its subsidiary Google. Born in Chennai, India, Pichai earned a degree in Metallurgical Engineering from the Indian Institute of Technology Kharagpur, followed by an MS from Stanford University and an MBA from the Wharton School.

Pichai joined Google in 2004, initially leading product management for Google Toolbar and later Chrome, which became the world's most popular web browser under his leadership. His successful work on Chrome and other projects led to his appointment as Google's CEO in 2015 and later as CEO of parent company Alphabet in 2019.

Under Pichai's guidance, Google has expanded its focus on artificial intelligence, cloud computing, and hardware development. He has played a crucial role in navigating the company through global challenges, balancing innovation with regulatory scrutiny. His leadership has cemented Google as one of the most influential tech companies globally.

A person who is happy is not because everything is right in his life, but because his attitude towards everything in his life is right.
—*The Economic Times, 2020*

It's important to follow your dreams and heart. Do something that excites you.
—*The Guardian, 2015*

We try to work on things which billions of people will use every day.
—*The New York Times, 2016*

You might fail a few times, but that's OK. You end up doing something worthwhile which you learn a great deal from.
—*Inc., 2018*

Wear your failure as a badge of honor.
—*Forbes, 2017*

It's always good to work with people who make you feel insecure about yourself. That way, you will constantly keep pushing your limits.
—*The Economic Times, 2019*

Let yourself feel insecure from time to time. It will help you grow as an individual.
—*Forbes, 2020*

In life don't react, always respond.
—*Business Insider, 2020*

— SUNDAR PICHAI

Susan Wojcicki

(CEO of YouTube)

Susan Wojcicki (1968-2024) was a prominent technology executive known for her pivotal role in YouTube's growth, a feat that has left an indelible mark on the digital landscape. After earning degrees from Harvard University, UC Santa Cruz, and UCLA, she began her career in marketing at Intel. Wojcicki joined Google in 1999 as its first marketing manager, playing a key role in the development of the company's early advertising models, including AdSense, which became a major revenue driver.

In 2006, Wojcicki advocated for Google's acquisition of YouTube, recognizing the platform's potential as a leading video-sharing service. Under her leadership as CEO starting in 2014, YouTube expanded dramatically, introducing new revenue streams like subscription services and premium content. Wojcicki also focused on improving content policies and balancing the platform's growth with responsibilities regarding misinformation and harmful content.

Throughout her career, Wojcicki was a strong advocate for women in technology, using her position to push for greater diversity and inclusion in the industry. Her strategic vision and leadership shaped YouTube into the world's largest video platform and influenced broader trends in digital media and online advertising.

Work smart. Get things done, and have fun.
—*Fortune, 2016*

It's important to be open-minded and willing to learn from others.
—*Business Insider, 2015*

Technology is an important enabler for creativity, but you also need to have the right culture.
—*Forbes, 2015*

It's really important to have a diversity of ideas and backgrounds to ensure that you're building the best product.
—*Vanity Fair, 2017*

If you follow your passion, you'll do great work. If you do great work, you'll have a great time.
—*Commencement speech at Johns Hopkins University, 2014*

Things are always changing, and companies need to recognize that and become comfortable with change.
—*Fast Company, 2017*

The most important thing for any company is to look to the future and not get stuck in the past.
—*The Wall Street Journal, 2015*

You need to have confidence in your ideas and enough perseverance to see them through.
—*Bloomberg, 2014*

— SUSAN WOJCICKI

Tim Cook

(CEO of Apple Inc.)

Tim Cook (born 1960) is an American business executive best known for leading Apple Inc. as CEO. Raised in Alabama, Cook earned a degree in industrial engineering from Auburn University and an MBA from Duke University. His early career included roles at IBM and Compaq, where he honed his expertise in supply chain management, a skill that would later prove critical at Apple.

Cook joined Apple in 1998, initially serving as Senior Vice President for Worldwide Operations. He was pivotal in optimizing Apple's supply chain, streamlining production, and increasing profit margins. This work helped Apple scale its operations globally and launch iconic products like the iPod, iPhone, and iPad. In 2011, Cook succeeded Steve Jobs as CEO, leading the company through its most significant period of growth.

Under Cook's leadership, Apple became the first publicly traded company to reach a trillion-dollar market cap. He has overseen the expansion of Apple's product line, including the Apple Watch and AirPods, and emphasized privacy, environmental sustainability, and corporate responsibility. Cook's steady hand and operational acumen have solidified Apple's status as a leader in the tech industry while also steering the company toward broader social goals.

Let your joy be in your journey—not in some distant goal.
—*Commencement speech at Auburn University, 2010*

We're not in the business of making the most. We're in the business of making the best.
—*Bloomberg, 2014*

If you're not doing some things that are crazy, then you're doing the wrong things.
—*Fast Company, 2016*

You want to be the pebble in the pond that creates the ripple for change.
—*People, 2015*

You can focus on things that are barriers, or you can focus on scaling the wall or redefining the problem.
—*Fast Company, 2014*

I think the most diverse group will produce the best product. I firmly believe that.
—*The New York Times, 2014*

There's no formula for business. You've got to be authentic and respect others.
—*Fortune, 2015*

We're going to give you things that you can't live without, that you just don't know you need today.
—*ABC News, 2014*

— TIM COOK

Walt Disney

(Co-founder of Disney Brothers Studio)

Walt Disney (1901–1966) was a visionary American entrepreneur, animator, and film producer who revolutionized the entertainment industry. Born in Chicago, Disney developed a passion for drawing at a young age and pursued a career in commercial art. In 1923, he co-founded the Disney Brothers Studio with his brother Roy, creating iconic characters like Mickey Mouse, who debuted in 1928's "Steamboat Willie". Mickey's success helped Disney pioneer synchronized sound in animation and set the stage for his future innovations.

In 1937, Disney released *Snow White and the Seven Dwarfs*, the first-ever full-length animated feature film, which became a massive success and established Disney as a leader in animation. He continued to push the boundaries of storytelling and technology with classics like *Pinocchio*, *Fantasia*, and *Bambi*. Disney also ventured into theme parks, opening Disneyland in 1955, which redefined family entertainment and became a cultural landmark.

Disney's relentless pursuit of excellence and innovation left a lasting legacy. His work transformed animation and film and laid the foundation for the global entertainment empire that continues to bear his name. Disney's influence on popular culture is unparalleled, and his creations continue to inspire generations.

I only hope that we never lose sight of one thing—that it was all started by a mouse.
—*Speech at Disneyland's 10th Anniversary, 1965*

The more you like yourself, the less you are like anyone else, which makes you unique.
—*Readers Digest, 1961*

You reach a point where you don't work for money.
—*The Saturday Evening Post, 1957*

The difference between winning and losing is most often not quitting.
—*The American Magazine, 1938*

Do what you do so well that they will want to see it again and bring their friends.
—*The New York Times, 1953*

We keep moving forward, opening new doors, and doing new things, because we're curious and curiosity keeps leading us down new paths.
—*Speech at the Disneyland Park opening, 1955*

Times and conditions change so rapidly that we must keep our aim constantly focused on the future.
—*Fortune, 1958*

All our dreams can come true, if we have the courage to pursue them.
—*Speech at the Disneyland Park opening, 1955*

— WALT DISNEY

Warren Buffett

(CEO of Berkshire Hathaway)

Warren Buffett (born 1930) is one of the most renowned investors and business magnates of the 20th and 21st centuries. Born in Omaha, Nebraska, Buffett demonstrated an early aptitude for numbers and finance, making his first stock purchase at 11. He studied under the legendary Benjamin Graham at Columbia University, where he honed the principles of value investing that would become the foundation of his career.

Buffett's significant achievement came through his transformative leadership of Berkshire Hathaway. He turned a struggling textile company into a diversified multinational conglomerate. Under his stewardship, Berkshire Hathaway acquired and invested in various successful businesses, including Coca-Cola, American Express, and Apple. His disciplined approach, focusing on the long term and picking companies with solid fundamentals, earned him the nickname "Oracle of Omaha".

Buffett has also been known for his philanthropy throughout his career. He committed to giving away most of his wealth through initiatives like the Giving Pledge, which he co-founded with Bill Gates. His investment strategies and business insights have made him a model for investors worldwide, emphasizing patience, discipline, and the power of compounding.

*Book Title

Price is what you pay, value is what you get.
—*The Essays of Warren Buffett, 1997

Risk comes from not knowing what you're doing.
—Forbes, 1994

The most important investment you can make is in yourself.
—The Motley Fool, 2018

Someone's sitting in the shade today because someone planted a tree a long time ago.
—The New York Times, 2006

Opportunities come infrequently. When it rains gold, put out the bucket, not the thimble.
—Letter to Berkshire Hathaway Shareholders, 2010

Be fearful when others are greedy, and be greedy when others are fearful.
—Berkshire Hathaway Shareholder Letter, 2004

You can't produce a baby in one month by getting nine women pregnant.
—*The Snowball, 2008

Diversification is protection against ignorance. It makes little sense if you know what you are doing.
—*The Essays of Warren Buffett, 1997

Honesty is a very expensive gift. Don't expect it from cheap people.
—*The Snowball, 2008

— WARREN BUFFETT

AUTHORS & EXPERTS

The pessimist complains about the wind. The optimist expects it to change. The leader adjusts the sails.

— JOHN C. MAXWELL

Amy Edmondson

(Author & Expert in Organizational Culture)

Amy Edmondson (born 1959) is a Harvard Business School professor known for her pioneering work on organizational psychology, specifically in the areas of leadership and teamwork. She has made significant contributions to understanding "psychological safety", a concept that explains how creating an environment where employees feel safe to speak up and take risks leads to better performance and innovation in organizations.

Her influential book *The Fearless Organization* (2018) highlights the importance of building workplaces where employees can freely share ideas without fear of retribution. This work has significantly impacted how modern companies approach leadership, particularly in fast-moving industries like tech, where innovation is critical. Edmondson's research emphasizes that open communication fosters better problem-solving and collaboration.

Edmondson's academic career is complemented by practical insights gained from her previous role as Chief Engineer at the renowned architect Buckminster Fuller's company. This blend of theoretical and real-world experience not only makes her a highly respected voice in both academic and corporate circles but also reassures leaders of the practical applicability of her theories, influencing them to rethink how they manage teams for better long-term success.

*Book Title

Psychological safety is not about being nice; it's about giving candid feedback, openly admitting mistakes, and learning from each other.
—*Administrative Science Quarterly, 1999*

In a psychologically safe environment, people feel free to speak up, share ideas, ask questions, and take risks without fear of embarrassment or punishment.
—*The Fearless Organization, 2018*

Mistakes are inevitable, but what really matters is how the team responds.
—*The Fearless Organization, 2018*

Innovation requires a workplace where it's safe to voice half-baked ideas, ask questions, and share concerns.
—*The Fearless Organization, 2018*

Teams that fail to create psychological safety end up avoiding risks, and that reduces their ability to innovate and succeed.
—*Harvard Business Review, 2019*

A culture of silence is a culture of missed opportunities.
—*The Fearless Organization, 2018*

The power of psychological safety is that it unlocks the potential of teams to achieve things that individuals cannot.
—*The Fearless Organization, 2018*

To thrive in uncertainty, people must be able to ask for help, admit failure, and challenge the status quo without fear of negative consequences.
—*TEDx Talk, 2019*

— AMY EDMONDSON

Brendon Burchard

(Author & Expert in Personal Fulfilment)

Brendon Burchard (born 1977) is a prominent author, high-performance coach, and motivational speaker known for his personal development and leadership work. He gained widespread recognition with his book *The Millionaire Messenger* (2011), which emphasizes the importance of turning personal knowledge into a successful business. The book quickly became a bestseller and established Burchard as a leading figure in the self-help industry.

Burchard's career trajectory was significantly altered by a life-altering car accident at the tender age of 19. This pivotal event prompted him to deeply ponder his life's purpose and the way he was living. The profound insights he gained from this experience ignited his enthusiasm for assisting others in realizing their full potential. This led to the creation of courses, seminars, and books that focus on productivity, motivation, and high performance. His book *High Performance Habits* (2017) delineates six scientifically proven habits that can propel individuals to excel in their personal and professional lives.

Beyond writing, Burchard founded the High Performance Academy and has been recognized by *Success Magazine* as one of the most influential leaders in personal growth. His work has impacted millions, with his online training programs and live events reaching audiences worldwide, solidifying his reputation as a top-tier motivational coach.

*Book Title

No matter how small you start, start something that matters.
—*The Motivation Manifesto, 2014*

Your destiny is ultimately controlled by the choices you make today.
—*The Charge, 2012*

Success and fulfillment come from your unrelenting belief in your ability to create and contribute.
—*High Performance Habits, 2017*

The time to have the map is before you enter the woods.
—*The Millionaire Messenger, 2011*

If you leave your growth to randomness, you'll always live in the land of mediocrity.
—*Blog post on BrendonBurchard.com, 2017*

You are not truly wealthy unless you are serving others in a way that feels aligned with your soul.
—*The Millionaire Messenger, 2011*

Greatness belongs to those who have mastered the ability to focus relentlessly on their ambitions and act decisively toward them.
—*The Charge, 2012*

Fear wins or freedom wins, and you get to decide.
—*The Motivation Manifesto, 2014*

Your past doesn't determine your future, but your patterns of thinking do.
—*The Brendon Show podcast, 2017*

— BRENDON BURCHARD

Brian Tracy

(Author & Expert in Growth Mindset)

Brian Tracy (born 1944) is a respected authority in the fields of personal development and business success. Born in Canada, he grew up facing economic challenges that drove him to start working at a young age. Tracy's early career was marked by a series of jobs, but it was in sales that he found his true calling. His determination and hard work quickly propelled him to the top, leading him to study the habits and strategies of successful people.

Tracy is best known for his work as a motivational speaker and author. He has written numerous books, with *Eat That Frog!* being one of the most popular. The book offers practical advice on overcoming procrastination and tackling the most challenging tasks first. His teachings cover a wide range of topics, including goal-setting, leadership, and personal effectiveness, making him a sought-after speaker and consultant for businesses around the world.

Throughout his career, Tracy has influenced millions through his seminars, books, and audio programs. His approach, which emphasizes practical strategies and self-discipline, has helped countless individuals and organizations improve their performance and achieve their goals. Tracy's legacy is one of empowerment, encouraging people to take control of their lives and strive for excellence.

*Book Title

Your ability to discipline yourself to set clear goals and then work toward them every day will do more to guarantee your success than any other single factor.
—*Goals!, 2003

The key to success is to focus our conscious mind on things we desire, not things we fear.
—*Change Your Thinking, Change Your Life, 2003

Successful people are always looking for opportunities to help others. Unsuccessful people are always asking, "What's in it for me?"
—*Maximum Achievement, 1993

The act of taking the first step is what separates the winners from the losers.
—*No Excuses!, 2010

Optimism is the one quality more associated with success and happiness than any other.
—*Maximum Achievement, 1993

There are no limits to what you can accomplish, except the limits you place on your own thinking.
—*The Psychology of Achievement, 1984

Your greatest asset is your earning ability. Your greatest resource is your time.
—*Eat That Frog!, 2001

Every minute you spend in planning saves 10 minutes in execution; this gives you a 1,000 percent Return on Energy!
—*Eat That Frog!, 2001

— BRIAN TRACY

Cal Newport

(Author & Expert in Productivity)

Cal Newport (born 1982) is an author, computer science professor, and productivity expert known for his influential work on deep work and digital minimalism. Raised in New Jersey, Newport excelled academically and pursued computer science at Dartmouth College, followed by a PhD from MIT. His academic background laid the foundation for exploring how focus and discipline can lead to high levels of achievement, both professionally and personally.

Newport gained widespread recognition with his 2016 book *Deep Work: Rules for Focused Success in a Distracted World*. The book argues that the ability to focus deeply is becoming increasingly rare and valuable in today's digital age. It offers practical strategies for cultivating deep work habits and resonates with a broad audience, from professionals seeking to improve productivity to students aiming for academic success. Newport's ideas challenge the conventional wisdom of multitasking and highlight the benefits of a more focused, intentional approach to work.

In addition to *Deep Work*, Newport is also known for his book *Digital Minimalism*, which advocates for a more mindful approach to technology use. As a professor at Georgetown University, he continues to research and write about the intersection of technology, productivity, and culture, influencing how people think about work-life balance in the modern era.

Book Title

The type of work that optimizes your performance is deep work. Shallow work doesn't tend to create much value in the world and is easy to replicate.
—*Deep Work, 2016

If you don't produce, you won't thrive—no matter how skilled or talented you are.
—*Deep Work, 2016

The key to developing a deep work habit is to move beyond good intentions and add routines and rituals to your working life.
—*Deep Work, 2016

If you can't learn, you can't thrive.
—*So Good They Can't Ignore You, 2012

You have a finite amount of willpower that becomes depleted as you use it. You must use it wisely.
—*Deep Work, 2016

The ability to perform deep work is becoming increasingly rare at exactly the same time it is becoming increasingly valuable in our economy.
—*Deep Work, 2016

Don't do small things repeatedly. Do great things, and make them solid and long-term.
—The New York Times, 2018

Discipline equals freedom when applied to a pursuit worth pursuing.
—The Tim Ferriss Show, 2017

— CAL NEWPORT

Carol Dweck

(Author & Expert in Growth Mindset)

Carol Dweck (born 1946) is a renowned psychologist best known for her groundbreaking work on the concept of mindset. A professor of psychology at Stanford University, she developed the theory of "fixed" and "growth" mindsets, which has profoundly influenced education, leadership, and personal development. Her research shows that individuals with a growth mindset—those who believe abilities can be developed—tend to achieve more success than those with a fixed mindset, who see abilities as static.

Dweck's work gained widespread recognition with the publication of her book *Mindset: The New Psychology of Success*. In it, she explains how fostering a growth mindset can lead to greater achievement in business, education, and beyond. The book has been widely embraced by educators, entrepreneurs, and leaders looking to improve motivation, resilience, and productivity within teams.

In addition to her academic achievements, Dweck has received numerous awards for her contributions to psychology, including the Distinguished Scientific Contribution Award from the American Psychological Association. Her research continues to influence the way individuals and organizations think about learning, talent development, and the power of believing in one's potential to grow and improve.

*Book Title

The view you adopt for yourself profoundly affects the way you lead your life.
—*Mindset, 2006*

Why waste time proving over and over how great you are, when you could be getting better?
—*Mindset, 2006*

In a growth mindset, challenges are exciting rather than threatening. So rather than thinking, "Oh, I'm going to reveal my weaknesses", you say, "Wow, here's a chance to grow".
—*Mindset, 2006*

People in a growth mindset don't just seek challenge, they thrive on it.
—*Mindset, 2006*

No matter what your ability is, effort is what ignites that ability and turns it into accomplishment.
—*Mindset, 2006*

Effort is one of those things that gives meaning to life. Effort means you care about something, that something is important to you and you are willing to work for it.
—*Mindset, 2006*

Leaders who embrace the growth mindset build teams that work well together, think creatively, and produce great results.
—*The Power of Believing You Can Improve (TED talk), 2014*

The hallmark of successful people is that they are always stretching themselves to learn new things.
—*Mindset, 2006*

— CAROL DWECK

Charles Duhigg

(Author & Expert in Productivity)

Charles Duhigg (born 1974) is an American journalist and author best known for his influential work on habits and productivity. After earning an MBA from Harvard Business School, Duhigg joined *The New York Times*, where his investigative reporting earned him numerous awards, including a Pulitzer Prize in 2013 for the series "The iEconomy", which explored the global economy's impact on American workers.

Duhigg gained widespread recognition with his 2012 book, *The Power of Habit: Why We Do What We Do in Life and Business*. The book delves into the science of habit formation and its applications in personal and professional contexts. It became a bestseller and sparked a broader conversation on how habits shape our lives, influencing everything from individual behavior to corporate strategies.

Following this success, Duhigg published *Smarter Faster Better* in 2016, which examines the science of productivity. Drawing on various case studies, Duhigg offers insights into how people and organizations can make better decisions, stay focused, and achieve more. Through his work, Duhigg has become a key figure in discussions about human behavior, providing readers with practical tools to improve their personal and professional lives.

*Book Title

Once you understand that habits can change, you have the freedom—and the responsibility—to remake them.
—*The Power of Habit, 2012

The difference between who you are and who you want to be is what you do.
—The Tim Ferriss Show podcast, 2016

Willpower isn't just a skill, it's a muscle, and like all muscles, it gets tired as it works harder, so there's less power left over for other things.
—*The Power of Habit, 2012

Small wins are exactly what they sound like, and are part of how keystone habits create widespread changes.
—*The Power of Habit, 2012

When people have a sense of control, they're more motivated, more productive, and happier.
—*Smarter Faster Better, 2016

The best way to get yourself motivated is to create a plan that makes tasks feel manageable and achievable.
—The Harvard Business Review, 2016

The secret to getting ahead is focusing on doing the most important thing first.
—The Tony Robbins Podcast, 2016

If you want to understand why you do what you do, you have to learn to identify the cues and rewards that drive your behavior.
—*The Power of Habit, 2012

— CHARLES DUHIGG

Chris Voss

(Author & Expert in Negotiation)

Chris Voss (born 1957) is a former FBI hostage negotiator turned business consultant, known for applying negotiation techniques to business and personal success. He served over 20 years with the FBI, where he became the lead international kidnapping negotiator. His field experience includes high-stakes negotiations in some of the world's most dangerous environments, dealing with terrorists, kidnappers, and criminals.

After leaving the FBI, Voss transitioned into teaching negotiation skills to business leaders and organizations. In 2016, he authored *Never Split the Difference*, a bestselling book outlining his negotiation approach, emphasizing empathy, active listening, and tactical questioning. His strategies challenge traditional negotiation methods, advocating for a more psychological approach to achieve desired outcomes.

Voss also founded The Black Swan Group, a consulting firm that trains individuals and companies in his unique negotiation techniques. His work has had a profound impact on business leaders, entrepreneurs, and negotiators across various industries, making him a sought-after speaker and coach in the field of negotiation.

*Book Title

When the pressure is on, you don't rise to the occasion—you fall to your highest level of preparation.
—*Never Split the Difference, 2016

He who has learned to disagree without being disagreeable has discovered the most valuable secret of negotiation.
—*Never Split the Difference, 2016

The most powerful word in negotiations is "fair".
—*Never Split the Difference, 2016

No deal is better than a bad deal.
—*Never Split the Difference, 2016

Use the "how" question as a means to say, "I care about what you're up against".
—Business Insider, 2017

In any negotiation, don't just pay attention to what the other person says. You need to listen to what they don't say as well.
—Forbes, 2019

Never be so sure of what you want that you wouldn't take something better.
—*Never Split the Difference, 2016

Great negotiators aim to make their counterpart feel safe, secure, and in control.
—*Never Split the Difference, 2016

The fastest way to getting someone to do something is to ask for help.
—*Never Split the Difference, 2016

— CHRIS VOSS

Clayton Christensen

(Author & Expert in Innovation)

Clayton Christensen (1952–2020) was a prominent American academic and business consultant best known for his theory of disruptive innovation. As a professor at Harvard Business School, Christensen's groundbreaking work in business strategy revolutionized how companies think about innovation. His 1997 book, *The Innovator's Dilemma*, outlined how smaller companies with fewer resources could challenge established firms by offering more straightforward, more affordable products or services. This concept continues to influence industries worldwide.

Christensen's disruptive innovation theory became a blueprint for understanding how technological advancements could displace market leaders. He showed how businesses could fail by focusing only on sustaining innovations, overlooking new technologies that appeal to different market segments. His ideas profoundly impacted technology companies, such as Apple and Intel, shaping how they approach competition and growth.

In addition to his work on innovation, Christensen made significant contributions to education and healthcare. His book *Disrupting Class* offered insights into how innovation could transform the educational system, and his research into healthcare focused on making the system more efficient and patient-centered. Christensen's thought leadership extended beyond business, leaving a legacy across various sectors.

*Book Title

Decide what you stand for. And then stand for it all the time.
—*Forbes*, 2012

The most important resource that you have is your time.
—*Harvard Business Review*, 2010

Resources are what you use to do things. Processes are how you make decisions. And priorities are why you make those decisions.
—*The Innovator's Dilemma*, 1997

You can talk all you want, but ultimately, people watch what you do.
—*How Will You Measure Your Life?*, 2012

When you have a hammer, everything looks like a nail. It's easy to apply what we know to every problem we face.
—*The Innovator's Solution*, 2003

If the decisions you make about where you invest your blood, sweat, and tears are not consistent with the person you aspire to be, you'll never become that person.
—*Harvard Business Review*, 2010

When the disruption is successful, disruption transforms a product that used to be expensive and complicated into something affordable and accessible.
—*Forbes*, 2012

Customers don't buy products; they hire them to do a job.
—*Competing Against Luck*, 2016

— CLAYTON CHRISTENSEN

AUTHORS & EXPERTS

Dale Carnegie

(Author & Expert in Communication)

Dale Carnegie (1888–1955) was an American writer and lecturer who became a pioneer in self-improvement and interpersonal communication. Born into poverty in Missouri, Carnegie worked as a salesman and aspiring actor before developing his public speaking courses. His breakthrough came in 1936 with the publication of *How to Win Friends and Influence People*, which has since become one of the best-selling books of all time.

Carnegie's work focused on practical advice for improving relationships and influencing others, especially in business and leadership. His principles, such as showing genuine interest in others and avoiding criticism, revolutionized how people approached communication. The book's timeless appeal has made it a cornerstone for individuals and organizations seeking to improve social dynamics and productivity.

Carnegie also founded the Dale Carnegie Institute, which has trained millions in leadership, sales, and communication skills. His other notable work, *How to Stop Worrying and Start Living* (1948), offered practical methods for reducing stress and improving mental well-being. Carnegie's legacy endures through his teachings, which remain widely applicable in personal and professional development.

*Book Title

Success is getting what you want. Happiness is wanting what you get.
—*How to Win Friends and Influence People, 1936*

Most of the important things in the world have been accomplished by people who have kept on trying when there seemed to be no hope at all.
—*How to Win Friends and Influence People, 1936*

You can make more friends in two months by becoming interested in other people than you can in two years by trying to get other people interested in you.
—*How to Win Friends and Influence People, 1936*

Remember, today is the tomorrow you worried about yesterday.
—*How to Stop Worrying and Start Living, 1948*

The successful man will profit from his mistakes and try again in a different way.
—*How to Win Friends and Influence People, 1936*

When dealing with people, remember you are not dealing with creatures of logic, but with creatures of emotion.
—*How to Win Friends and Influence People, 1936*

Don't be afraid of enemies who attack you. Be afraid of the friends who flatter you.
—*How to Win Friends and Influence People, 1936*

Action breeds confidence and courage. If you want to conquer fear, do not sit home and think about it. Go out and get busy.
—*How to Stop Worrying and Start Living, 1948*

— DALE CARNEGIE

Daniel Kahneman

(Author & Expert in Decision-making)

Daniel Kahneman (1934-2024) was a psychologist whose groundbreaking work reshaped the fields of economics and decision-making. Born in Tel Aviv, he spent his childhood in France before moving to Israel. He later earned a PhD in psychology from the University of California, Berkeley. Kahneman's early work in cognitive psychology laid the foundation for his future exploration of how people make decisions under uncertainty.

In collaboration with Amos Tversky, Kahneman developed *prospect theory*, a cornerstone of behavioral economics. This theory challenged the traditional economic belief that people make rational decisions based on self-interest. Instead, it demonstrated that cognitive biases, emotions, and irrationality often influence human choices. Their work highlighted concepts like "loss aversion", which explains why people fear losses more than they value gains of the same size.

In 2002, Kahneman was awarded the Nobel Prize in Economic Sciences for his contributions, despite not being an economist by training. His book *Thinking, Fast and Slow* (2011) further popularized his ideas, making them accessible to a broader audience. Today, Kahneman's research continues to influence economics, psychology, and business strategy, particularly in areas related to decision-making, risk, and behavioral finance.

Book Title

The confidence people have in their beliefs is not a measure of the quality of evidence but of the coherence of the story that the mind has managed to construct.
—*Thinking, Fast and Slow, 2011*

We can be blind to the obvious, and we are also blind to our blindness.
—*Thinking, Fast and Slow, 2011*

Nothing in life is as important as you think it is, while you are thinking about it.
—*Thinking, Fast and Slow, 2011*

Optimistic overconfidence is the engine of capitalism.
—*Thinking, Fast and Slow, 2011*

What you see is all there is.
—*Thinking, Fast and Slow, 2011*

The idea that the future is unpredictable is undermined every day by the ease with which the past is explained.
—*Thinking, Fast and Slow, 2011*

A reliable way of making people believe in falsehoods is frequent repetition, because familiarity is not easily distinguished from truth.
—*Thinking, Fast and Slow, 2011*

The illusion that we understand the past fosters overconfidence in our ability to predict the future.
—*Thinking, Fast and Slow, 2011*

— DANIEL KAHNEMAN

Daniel Pink

(Author & Expert in Motivation)

Daniel Pink (born 1964) is a bestselling author and influential business and behavioral science thinker. After earning a degree in linguistics from Northwestern University and a law degree from Yale, Pink chose an unconventional career path, opting to work as a speechwriter for Vice President Al Gore before transitioning into writing full-time.

Pink gained widespread recognition with his book *Drive: The Surprising Truth About What Motivates Us* (2009), where he challenges traditional views on motivation by emphasizing autonomy, mastery, and purpose as key drivers of performance. His work, praised for its accessible style and deep insights, has helped individuals and organizations rethink how they approach motivation and productivity, validating his influence in the field.

In addition to *Drive*, Pink's other notable works include *A Whole New Mind* (2005), which explores the importance of right-brain thinking in a rapidly changing world, and *When: The Scientific Secrets of Perfect Timing* (2018), which examines the best times to make decisions and perform tasks. His books have been translated into dozens of languages, making him a global voice in the conversation on work and human behavior. Pink's ideas have profoundly impacted business practices, education, and personal development.

*Book Title

The secret to high performance and satisfaction—at work, at school, and at home—is the deeply human need to direct our own lives, to learn and create new things, and to do better by ourselves and our world.
—*Drive, 2009

Management isn't about walking around and seeing if people are in their offices. It's about creating conditions for people to do their best work.
—*Drive, 2009

Control leads to compliance; autonomy leads to engagement.
—*Drive, 2009

Autonomy, mastery, and purpose are what drive people.
—*Drive, 2009

Timing is really a science—it's not an art. You can make better decisions based on science about when to do things.
—*When, 2018

The capacity to sell isn't some unnatural adaptation to the merciless world of commerce. It's part of who we are.
—*To Sell Is Human, 2012

Empathy is about standing in someone else's shoes, feeling with his or her heart, seeing with his or her eyes. Not only is empathy hard to outsource and automate, but it makes the world a better place.
—*A Whole New Mind, 2005

You can't lead others until you can lead yourself.
—Forbes, 2011

— DANIEL PINK

Darren Hardy

(Author & Expert in Growth Mindset)

Darren Hardy (born 1971) is an influential author, keynote speaker, and former publisher of *Success* magazine. Hardy began his career as an entrepreneur at a young age, founding his first business before age 20. His early success in real estate and other ventures made him a respected personal development and business leadership figure.

Hardy's influence extends globally through his bestselling book, *The Compound Effect*, which illustrates how small, consistent actions can lead to significant results over time. This book has struck a chord with readers worldwide, offering practical strategies for personal and professional growth. His other work, *The Entrepreneur Roller Coaster*, tackles the challenges of starting and growing a business, resonating with entrepreneurs across the globe.

Beyond his writing, Hardy has impacted the lives of millions through his speaking engagements, workshops, and online training programs. His work emphasizes the importance of discipline, perseverance, and continuous learning, making him a key figure for those looking to achieve long-term success in their careers and personal lives.

*Book Title

Consistency is the ultimate key to success. Yet it's one of the ultimate pitfalls for people who are struggling to achieve.
—*The Compound Effect, 2010*

The person who has a clear, compelling, and white-hot burning why will always defeat even the best of the best at how.
—*Success Magazine, 2016*

You alone are responsible for what you do, don't do, or how you respond to what's done to you.
—*The Compound Effect, 2010*

Small, smart choices, when consistently applied, lead to radical differences in results.
—*The Compound Effect, 2010*

Your biggest challenge isn't that you've intentionally been making bad choices. Your biggest challenge is that you've been sleepwalking through your choices.
—*The Compound Effect, 2010*

You will never change your life until you change something you do daily. The secret of your success is found in your daily routine.
—*Entrepreneur on Fire podcast, 2015*

Choices are at the root of every one of your results. Each choice starts a behavior that over time becomes a habit.
—*The Compound Effect, 2010*

Motivation without action leads to self-delusion.
—*The Darren Hardy Show, 2016*

— DARREN HARDY

Dave Ramsey

(Author & Expert in Finance)

Dave Ramsey (born 1960) is a personal finance expert, radio host, and author renowned for his straightforward advice on debt cuts and financial management. Raised in Antioch, Tennessee, Ramsey built a real estate portfolio in his twenties, only to lose it all during the 1980s due to excessive debt. This experience led him to study personal finance extensively and develop his debt-free philosophy.

Ramsey's significant achievement is his financial counselling empire, built around *The Dave Ramsey Show*, a widely syndicated radio program where he offers practical advice on budgeting, saving, and eliminating debt. He also created the "7 Baby Steps", a step-by-step plan designed to help individuals achieve financial security. His book *The Total Money Makeover* has sold millions of copies, guiding readers through the process of getting out of debt and building wealth.

In addition to his media presence, Ramsey founded Ramsey Solutions, which provides financial education and resources, including courses like Financial Peace University. His approach, which emphasizes living within one's means, avoiding debt, and saving for the future, has helped millions regain control of their finances and build a solid financial foundation.

*Book Title

You must gain control over your money or the lack of it will forever control you.
—*The Total Money Makeover, 2003*

A budget is telling your money where to go instead of wondering where it went.
—*Financial Peace Revisited, 2002*

People who change their lives change their daily habits.
—*The Total Money Makeover, 2003*

Success is a pile of failure that you are standing on.
—*EntreLeadership, 2011*

Fear is the enemy of hope.
—*EntreLeadership, 2011*

Earning a lot of money is not the key to prosperity. How you handle it is.
—*The Total Money Makeover, 2003*

You've got to tell your money what to do or it will leave.
—*The Total Money Makeover, 2003*

We buy things we don't need with money we don't have to impress people we don't like.
—*Financial Peace Revisited, 2002*

The borrower is slave to the lender.
—*The Total Money Makeover, 2003*

A goal without a plan is just a dream.
—*EntreLeadership, 2011*

— DAVE RAMSEY

David Allen

(Author & Expert in Productivity)

David Allen (born 1945) is a productivity expert, author, and consultant best known for creating the "Getting Things Done" (GTD) methodology. Born in Louisiana, Allen's career path included a variety of jobs, from magician to karate instructor, before he found his true calling in the field of productivity. His diverse experiences laid the groundwork for his later work, where he sought to help people manage their tasks and reduce stress.

Allen's most significant contribution is his 2001 book, *Getting Things Done: The Art of Stress-Free Productivity.* The GTD method, which emphasizes capturing all tasks and ideas in a reliable system, breaking them down into actionable steps, and regularly reviewing progress, became a global phenomenon. This approach, adopted by millions worldwide, from corporate executives to creative professionals, has created a global community of individuals striving for stress-free productivity.

In addition to writing, Allen founded the David Allen Company, offering training and consulting services to individuals and organizations looking to improve productivity. His work has had a lasting impact on how people approach work and personal tasks, promoting a clear mind and organized approach to achieving goals. Allen continues to be a leading voice in productivity, inspiring others to live and work more efficiently.

Book Title

Your mind is for having ideas, not holding them.
—*Getting Things Done, 2001*

You can do anything, but not everything.
—*Success Magazine, 2009*

Much of the stress that people feel doesn't come from having too much to do. It comes from not finishing what they started.
—*Getting Things Done, 2001*

If you don't pay appropriate attention to what has your attention, it will take more of your attention than it deserves.
—*Getting Things Done, 2001*

It does not take much strength to do things, but it requires a great deal of strength to decide what to do.
—*Fast Company, 2011*

You can only feel good about what you're not doing when you know what you're not doing.
—*Getting Things Done, 2001*

Things rarely get stuck because of lack of time. They get stuck because the doing of them has not been defined.
—*Getting Things Done, 2001*

The secret of getting ahead is getting started.
—*The New York Times, 2012*

When you start to make things happen, you really begin to believe that you can make things happen. And that makes things happen.
—*Forbes, 2013*

— DAVID ALLEN

Edward de Bono

(Author & Expert in Problem-solving)

Edward de Bono (1933-2021) was a Maltese thinker whose ideas on creative problem-solving revolutionized how businesses approach challenges. Trained in medicine and psychology, de Bono studied at the University of Malta and later at Oxford University. He drew on his diverse academic background to question conventional thinking methods, ultimately developing new approaches to innovation.

In 1967, de Bono coined the term "lateral thinking", advocating for an unconventional approach to problem-solving. He believed that traditional, linear thinking limited creativity. His breakthrough work, *The Use of Lateral Thinking*, became widely recognized in business and education, where it helped people break away from ingrained patterns and think more creatively.

De Bono's influence extended through his more than 85 published books, including *Six Thinking Hats*—a framework for improving group discussions and decision-making. He worked as a consultant for major companies and governments, leaving a lasting impact on leadership and organizational strategy by promoting out-of-the-box thinking. His legacy is one of intellectual curiosity and practical tools for fostering innovation.

*Book Title

Creativity involves breaking out of established patterns in order to look at things in a different way.
—*Lateral Thinking, 1970*

You cannot dig a hole in a different place by digging the same hole deeper.
—*Lateral Thinking, 1970*

It is well known that 'problem solving' is largely reactive, while creativity is proactive.
—*Serious Creativity, 1992*

Dealing with complexity is an inefficient and unnecessary waste of time, attention, and mental energy. Simplicity is the ultimate sophistication.
—*Simplicity, 1998*

Lateral thinking is concerned not with playing with the existing pieces but with seeking to change those very pieces.
—*The Use of Lateral Thinking, 1967*

Many highly intelligent people are poor thinkers. Many people of average intelligence are skilled thinkers. The power of a car is separate from the way the car is driven.
—*Six Thinking Hats, 1985*

To get new answers, you have to ask new questions.
—*Lateral Thinking, 1970*

There is a need to use creative thinking to open up new possibilities and to approach problems from new directions.
—*Lateral Thinking, 1970*

— EDWARD DE BONO

Eric Ries

(Author & Expert in Innovation)

Eric Ries (born 1978) is an American entrepreneur and author best known for pioneering the Lean Startup methodology, revolutionizing how startups and businesses approach innovation and growth. After studying computer science at Yale, Ries co-founded the IMVU social network in 2004, where he began applying lean principles to software development and business management. His experiences there laid the foundation for his later work.

In 2011, Ries published *The Lean Startup*, a bestselling book that introduced concepts like "validated learning", "minimum viable product", and rapid iteration. These ideas advocate for testing assumptions quickly and using customer feedback to adapt, reducing waste in both time and resources. The methodology has been widely adopted not only by startups but also by large corporations seeking to maintain agility in a competitive market.

Ries went on to found the Long-Term Stock Exchange (LTSE) to help companies focus on sustainable growth rather than short-term profits. His work has impacted entrepreneurial ecosystems worldwide, influencing how businesses think about product development, scalability, and customer-centric approaches. Ries continues to be an influential voice in business, advising companies and speaking on innovation.

*Book Title

A startup is a human institution designed to create a new product or service under conditions of extreme uncertainty.
—*The Lean Startup, 2011

The only way to win is to learn faster than anyone else.
—*The Lean Startup, 2011

Success is not delivering a feature; success is learning how to solve the customer's problem.
—Business Insider, 2011

Innovation is a bottoms-up, decentralized, and unpredictable thing, but that doesn't mean it cannot be managed.
—*The Lean Startup, 2011

Entrepreneurship is a management science.
—*The Lean Startup, 2011

The lesson of the Lean Startup is that you can't trade learning for growth.
—Forbes, 2013

Build-measure-learn is a framework to guide thinking. It helps startups make progress under conditions of extreme uncertainty.
—*The Lean Startup, 2011

If we do not know who the customer is, we do not know what quality is.
—*The Lean Startup, 2011

In a startup, no facts exist inside the building, only opinions.
—Harvard Business Review, 2011

— ERIC RIES

Gary Vaynerchuk

(Author & Expert in Marketing)

Gary Vaynerchuk (born 1975) is a Belarusian-American entrepreneur, author, and internet personality known for his pioneering work in digital marketing and social media. He first gained prominence as the co-founder of VaynerMedia, a digital agency that has worked with Fortune 500 companies to build their online presence. His journey into the business world began by transforming his family's liquor store into a multimillion-dollar e-commerce platform, Wine Library.

Vaynerchuk leveraged the power of YouTube and social media early on, launching *Wine Library TV*, a daily video blog that helped him establish a solid personal brand. This success propelled him into digital marketing, where he became an expert in understanding consumer behavior and leveraging emerging platforms to build businesses.

In addition to his work with VaynerMedia, Vaynerchuk is a prolific author, having written several bestselling books on entrepreneurship, marketing, and personal branding. He is also a sought-after speaker and angel investor, with early investments in companies like Twitter, Facebook, and Uber. His no-nonsense approach to business and emphasis on hustle and perseverance have inspired a generation of entrepreneurs and marketers.

Book Title

> Skills are cheap. Passion is priceless.
> —*Crush It!, 2009

> If you're not putting out relevant content in relevant places, you don't exist.
> —*Jab, Jab, Jab, Right Hook, 2013

> The best marketing strategy ever: Care.
> —The Breakfast Club, 2016

> Your legacy is being written by yourself. Make the right decisions.
> —*#AskGaryVee, 2016

> There's no reason to do things you hate. None.
> —*Crush It!, 2009

> You can't scale caring.
> —*The Thank You Economy, 2011

> Look yourself in the mirror and ask yourself, "What do I want to do every day for the rest of my life"? Do that.
> —*Crush It!, 2009

> It's never a bad time to start a business unless you're starting a mediocre business.
> —GaryVee blog post, 2017

> The truth is that finding happiness in what you do every day is so imperative.
> —The Tim Ferriss Show, 2014

— GARY VAYNERCHUK

Grant Cardone

(Author & Expert in Sales)

Grant Cardone (born 1958) is an American entrepreneur, real estate investor, and motivational speaker known for his sales and business growth expertise. Raised in Lake Charles, Louisiana, Cardone faced early hardships, including losing his father at a young age, which fueled his determination to succeed. After earning a degree in accounting, he entered the world of sales, quickly establishing himself as a top performer.

Cardone is best known for building a multi-billion-dollar real estate portfolio through his company, Cardone Capital, which manages thousands of apartment units across the U.S. He is also the author of several best-selling books, including *The 10X Rule* and *Sell or Be Sold*, where he shares his insights on how to achieve massive success by taking relentless action and thinking big. His "10X" philosophy encourages individuals and businesses to multiply their efforts to reach their highest potential.

In addition to his real estate and publishing ventures, Cardone runs Grant Cardone Enterprises, offering sales training and business consulting services. His energetic speaking style and no-nonsense advice have made him a popular figure in the self-improvement and entrepreneurial worlds, where he motivates millions through his seminars, online courses, and social media presence.

*Book Title

Success is your duty, obligation, and responsibility.
—*The 10X Rule, 2011*

Your greatness is limited only by the investments you make in yourself.
—*Be Obsessed or Be Average, 2016*

Set no targets and you will get nowhere.
—*The 10X Rule, 2011*

You will not have a successful life surrounded by negative people.
—*Sell or Be Sold, 2012*

You sleep like you're rich... I'm up like I'm broke.
—*Twitter, 2017*

Approach every situation with a whatever-it-takes mindset.
—*The 10X Rule, 2011*

Your problem isn't the problem. Your reaction is the problem.
—*Sell or Be Sold, 2012*

To get to the next level of whatever you're doing, you must think and act in a wildly different way than you previously have been.
—*The 10X Rule, 2011*

Do what others refuse to do.
—*Be Obsessed or Be Average, 2016*

Never lower your target; increase your actions.
—*The 10X Rule, 2011*

— GRANT CARDONE

Gretchen Rubin

(Author & Expert in Motivation)

Gretchen Rubin (born 1965) is an American author and speaker known for her work on happiness, habits, and human nature. She began her career as a lawyer, clerking for Supreme Court Justice Sandra Day O'Connor, before pivoting to writing, where she found her true passion. Rubin gained widespread recognition with her 2009 book *The Happiness Project*, which chronicles her year-long experiment to test various theories about how to live a happier life.

Following *The Happiness Project*'s success, Rubin continued to explore themes of personal development and well-being in her subsequent books, including *Happier at Home* and *Better Than Before*. Her work emphasizes practical strategies for a fulfilling life, focusing on understanding individual tendencies and creating habits that lead to lasting happiness. She also developed the "Four Tendencies" framework, which categorizes people based on how they respond to expectations, a concept that has resonated with a broad audience.

In addition to her writing, Rubin hosts the popular *Happier* podcast with her sister, Elizabeth Craft, where they discuss insights on happiness and habit formation. Rubin's work has made her a leading voice in the personal development field, helping millions of people cultivate more meaningful and joyful lives.

*Book Title

What you do every day matters more than what you do once in a while.
—*The Happiness Project, 2009*

To be happy, we need to think about feeling good, feeling bad, and feeling right, in an atmosphere of growth.
—*The Happiness Project, 2009*

Outer order contributes to inner calm.
—*Outer Order, Inner Calm, 2019*

By doing a little bit each day, you can get a lot accomplished.
—*Better Than Before, 2015*

Habits are the invisible architecture of daily life.
—*Better Than Before, 2015*

The biggest waste of time is to do well something that we need not do at all.
—Blog post on *The Happiness Project, 2011*

It's easy to be heavy; hard to be light.
—*The Happiness Project, 2009*

Enthusiasm is more important to mastery than innate talent.
—*The Happiness Project, 2009*

Work can be one of the most rewarding aspects of life, but success means different things to different people.
—*Forbes, 2014*

The days are long, but the years are short.
—*The Happiness Project, 2009*

— GRETCHEN RUBIN

Hal Elrod

(Author & Expert in Growth Mindset)

Hal Elrod (born 1979) is an American author, speaker, and success coach best known for his book *The Miracle Morning*. His life took a dramatic turn at the age of 20 when he was involved in a near-fatal car accident, leaving him with severe injuries and a prognosis that he might never walk again. Defying the odds, Elrod walked again and ran a 52-mile ultra-marathon, inspiring others with his story of resilience and determination.

Elrod's breakthrough came with the publication of *The Miracle Morning* in 2012, a book that has since sold over a million copies and been translated into multiple languages. The book introduces a morning routine known as "SAVERS" (Silence, Affirmations, Visualization, Exercise, Reading, and Scribing), which has helped millions of readers transform their lives by starting their days with purpose and intention. His work emphasizes personal development and the power of daily habits in achieving long-term success.

Beyond writing, Elrod is a sought-after keynote speaker and the host of *The Achieve Your Goals* podcast, where he shares insights on productivity, goal setting, and living a fulfilled life. His influence extends across a global community dedicated to personal growth and achieving extraordinary results.

*Book Title

The moment you take responsibility for everything in your life is the moment you can change anything in your life.
—*The Miracle Morning, 2012

Love the life you have while you create the life of your dreams.
—Blog post on HalElrod.com, 2016

Let today be the day you give up who you've been for who you can become.
—*The Miracle Morning, 2012

You are where you are because of who you were, but where you go depends entirely on who you choose to be.
—The School of Greatness podcast, 2016

The purpose of a goal is not to reach the goal, it's to become the person who can accomplish any goal.
—Blog post on HalElrod.com, 2017

You can't improve your life until you improve yourself.
—*The Miracle Equation, 2019

Mediocrity doesn't happen overnight. Excellence doesn't happen overnight. Every single day matters.
—*The Miracle Morning, 2012

Success is not something you pursue. Success is something you attract by the person you become.
—*The Miracle Morning, 2012

Wake up every day with a purpose and take massive action toward your goals.
—*The Miracle Morning, 2012

— HAL ELROD

Harold Kerzner

(Author & Expert in Project Management)

Harold Kerzner (born 1940) is a renowned project management expert known for his influential work in advancing modern project management techniques. With a background in engineering, Kerzner earned his PhD in engineering and business from the University of Illinois. He has been a prominent figure in academia and industry, focusing on the principles that make projects successful in various sectors.

Kerzner's most notable contribution is his bestselling book *Project Management: A Systems Approach to Planning, Scheduling, and Controlling*, a standard reference for project managers worldwide. In it, he emphasizes the importance of aligning projects with organizational goals and introduces the concept of project management maturity, helping businesses assess and improve their project management capabilities.

Throughout his career, Kerzner has worked with companies worldwide, delivering seminars and consulting services that focus on improving project outcomes. His work has significantly shaped how organizations approach project management, particularly in balancing scope, time, and cost. His legacy includes not only his written contributions but also the Kerzner International Project Manager of the Year Award, which honors excellence in the field of project management.

*Book Title

Project management is not about managing projects; it's about leading people to successful outcomes.
—*Project Management, 2017*

If project management is to succeed, then it must become an integral part of the organization's culture.
—*Project Management Best Practices, 2013*

The essence of project management is the ability to foresee problems before they happen, to plan, organize, and control activities so that the project is completed successfully in spite of all the risks.
—*Project Management, 2017*

Companies make the mistake of thinking that just because their employees are technically skilled, they automatically know how to manage a project.
—*Project Management, 2017*

Communication is the key to success in project management, and lack of communication is the main reason why projects fail.
—*Project Management, 2017*

Projects are the engines that drive organizational growth and innovation.
—*Innovation Project Management, 2019*

Successful project management is about learning from past mistakes and applying those lessons to future projects.
—*Project Management Case Studies, 2017*

— HAROLD KERZNER

Ivan Misner

(Author & Expert in Networking)

Ivan Misner (born 1956) is an American entrepreneur and author best known for founding Business Network International (BNI) in 1985. BNI grew to become one of the world's largest business networking organizations, with chapters across the globe, helping professionals connect, exchange referrals, and build relationships that drive business growth. Misner's concept of structured networking has transformed how professionals build their networks and leverage connections for business success.

Misner's contributions extend beyond BNI. He has written numerous books, including *Networking Like a Pro* and *The World's Best Known Marketing Secret*, where he shares effective networking and relationship-building strategies. His teachings emphasize the importance of "giver's gain", the idea that helping others succeed creates opportunities for your own growth. This philosophy has become a cornerstone of BNI's global success.

A respected thought leader, Misner holds a PhD in organizational behavior and continues influencing the business world through his speaking engagements, publications, and podcasts. His work has helped entrepreneurs and professionals understand that personal connections and trusted relationships are critical components of business success, making him a key figure in the world of networking and business development.

*Book Title

Networking is more about farming than it is about hunting.
—*The 29% Solution, 2007*

Givers gain: When you give business to others, you will get business in return.
—*BNI's Core Philosophy, 1998*

The secret to successful networking is to make it about the other person.
—*Blog post on IvanMisner.com, 2016*

Networking is not about collecting contacts; it's about planting relationships.
—*BNI.com, 2016*

Networking is a marathon, not a sprint.
—*Networking Like a Pro, 2010*

Visibility plus credibility equals profitability.
—*Masters of Networking, 2005*

The foundation of networking is the law of reciprocity.
—*Entrepreneur, 2011*

Don't underestimate the power of a good network; it can open doors that you might not even know exist.
—*Forbes, 2013*

Networking is not a numbers game; it's a people game.
—*The 29% Solution, 2007*

Trust is built with consistency.
—*Blog post on IvanMisner.com, 2017*

— IVAN MISNER

James Clear

(Author & Expert in Productivity)

James Clear (born 1986) is an author, entrepreneur, and speaker best known for his habit formation and personal development expertise. Raised in Ohio, Clear's early interest in sports and self-improvement was catalyzed by a severe injury in high school, which left him with a shattered skull. The recovery process taught him the importance of small, consistent actions, a theme that would become central to his work.

Clear's most notable achievement is his book *Atomic Habits*, published in 2018. The book quickly became a bestseller, praised for its practical and actionable approach to building good habits and breaking bad ones. Clear's argument that when consistently applied, tiny changes can lead to significant improvements over time is a powerful tool for personal development. His work combines scientific research with real-world examples, making complex behavioral psychology accessible to a broad audience.

In addition to his writing, Clear is a sought-after speaker and has collaborated with organizations ranging from Fortune 500 companies to professional sports teams. His insights on productivity, decision-making, and continuous improvement have impacted how individuals and businesses approach success. Through his writing and speaking, Clear continues to influence a global audience, helping people achieve their goals by mastering the art of habit formation.

Book Title

You do not rise to the level of your goals. You fall to the level of your systems.
—*Atomic Habits, 2018*

Habits are the compound interest of self-improvement.
—*Atomic Habits, 2018*

Every action you take is a vote for the type of person you wish to become.
—*Atomic Habits, 2018*

Success is the product of daily habits—not once-in-a-lifetime transformations.
—*Atomic Habits, 2018*

You should be far more concerned with your current trajectory than with your current results.
—*Atomic Habits, 2018*

Goals are good for setting a direction, but systems are best for making progress.
—*Atomic Habits, 2018*

Be the designer of your world and not merely the consumer of it.
—*Atomic Habits, 2018*

The most effective way to change your habits is to focus not on what you want to achieve, but on who you wish to become.
—*Atomic Habits, 2018*

Small habits don't add up. They compound.
—*Atomic Habits, 2018*

— JAMES CLEAR

AUTHORS & EXPERTS

Jeanne Bliss

(Author & Expert in Customer Focus)

Jeanne Bliss (born 1950) is a pioneer in customer experience and a leader in transforming businesses into customer-centric organizations. With over 35 years of experience, Bliss has held leadership roles at major companies like Lands' End, Allstate, and Microsoft, where she served as the first-ever Chief Customer Officer (CCO). Her work has focused on creating meaningful, long-term relationships between companies and their customers.

Bliss founded CustomerBliss, a consulting firm that helps businesses achieve customer loyalty and growth through improved customer experience strategies. She is also a best-selling author, with notable books like *Chief Customer Officer* and *Would You Do That to Your Mother?*, which provide insights into building businesses that customers love and trust.

Her influence has extended beyond individual companies. Bliss co-founded the Customer Experience Professionals Association (CXPA), setting the standard for the growing field of customer experience management. Throughout her career, she has been instrumental in shaping how companies view and treat their customers, fostering a culture of accountability and empathy at every business level.

*Book Title

Companies that earn admirable customer experiences make a decision that they will grow differently.
—*Chief Customer Officer, 2006*

Customers are not metrics. They are human beings with lives that you either improve or get in the way of.
—*Would You Do That to Your Mother?, 2018*

The key to successful customer experience transformation is understanding that this is a journey, not a project.
—*Chief Customer Officer 2.0, 2015*

It's not about making more promises, it's about keeping the ones you've already made.
—*I Love You More Than My Dog, 2011*

Companies that will thrive in the future are those that not only think about the bottom line but also about how they impact customers' lives.
—*Chief Customer Officer, 2006*

Make customer experience your best habit, not a new initiative.
—*Chief Customer Officer 2.0, 2015*

Decide to care about your customers and how your business shows up in their lives.
—*Would You Do That to Your Mother?, 2018*

Be deliberate about the memories you create for your customers.
—*I Love You More Than My Dog, 2011*

— JEANNE BLISS

John C. Maxwell

(Author & Expert in Leadership)

John C. Maxwell (born 1947) is a leading authority on leadership and personal development. He began his career as a pastor, gaining firsthand experience managing teams and guiding communities. His passion for leadership eventually led him to write and speak extensively on the subject, shaping how organizations and individuals think about influence and personal growth.

Maxwell has authored numerous bestselling books, including *The 21 Irrefutable Laws of Leadership* and *The 5 Levels of Leadership*. His practical insights on leadership have resonated with readers worldwide, and his books have sold millions of copies. Beyond writing, Maxwell founded EQUIP, a nonprofit organization that has trained millions of leaders in over 180 countries.

Maxwell's influence spans the corporate world, government, and education. He has been recognized as one of the world's foremost leadership thinkers and has consulted for Fortune 500 companies. Through his books, speeches, and leadership programs, John C. Maxwell has profoundly impacted how leaders are developed, with a strong emphasis on character, integrity, and service.

*Book Title

A leader is one who knows the way, goes the way, and shows the way.
—*The 21 Irrefutable Laws of Leadership, 1998*

The pessimist complains about the wind. The optimist expects it to change. The leader adjusts the sails.
—*Developing the Leader Within You, 1993*

Leadership is not about titles, positions, or flowcharts. It is about one life influencing another.
—*Becoming a Person of Influence, 1997*

You don't overcome challenges by making them smaller but by making yourself bigger.
—*How Successful People Think, 2009*

A leader's potential is determined by those closest to him.
—*The 21 Irrefutable Laws of Leadership, 1998*

The greatest mistake we make is living in constant fear that we will make one.
—*Failing Forward, 2000*

Leaders must be close enough to relate to others, but far enough ahead to motivate them.
—*The 21 Irrefutable Laws of Leadership, 1998*

Change is inevitable. Growth is optional.
—*The 15 Invaluable Laws of Growth, 2012*

A good leader is a person who takes a little more than his share of the blame and a little less than his share of the credit.
—*Leadership Gold, 2008*

— JOHN C. MAXWELL

AUTHORS & EXPERTS

Keith Ferrazzi

(Author & Expert in Networking)

Keith Ferrazzi (born 1966) is an American entrepreneur and author widely recognized for his expertise in networking and relationship-building. He earned his MBA from Harvard Business School and started his career in marketing with leadership roles at Deloitte and Starwood Hotels. Ferrazzi's early career was marked by his ability to form strong professional connections, a skill that would become the foundation of his later work.

In 2005, Ferrazzi published *Never Eat Alone*, a bestselling book that explores the power of networking and how building authentic relationships can accelerate personal and professional success. His advice to never dine alone but instead use meals as opportunities to connect with others became a guiding principle for many business professionals. His work emphasizes generosity, authenticity, and the idea that success is a group effort rather than an individual pursuit.

Ferrazzi is also the founder and CEO of Ferrazzi Greenlight, a research and consulting firm that helps organizations improve teamwork, leadership, and performance. His approach to business focuses on collaboration and the power of positive relationships, influencing how companies foster productivity and engagement in the workplace.

Book Title

Success in any field, but especially in business, is about working with people, not against them.
—*Never Eat Alone, 2005*

The currency of real networking is not greed but generosity.
—*Never Eat Alone, 2005*

In business, relationships are the most important assets.
—*Who's Got Your Back, 2009*

Your network is your destiny. The people you surround yourself will shape your future.
—*Never Eat Alone, 2005*

It's not what you know or even who you know, but how well you know them that really counts.
—*Never Eat Alone, 2005*

Success isn't a solo endeavor. It's a team effort. We all need a little help to achieve our goals.
—*Who's Got Your Back, 2009*

You can't get there alone. And your network – your friends, family, and associates – will determine where you go.
—*Never Eat Alone, 2005*

Be generous, and the favor will return to you a hundredfold.
—*Never Eat Alone, 2005*

Vulnerability and honesty are the foundation for building trust and deeper relationships in business.
—*Who's Got Your Back, 2009*

— KEITH FERRAZZI

AUTHORS & EXPERTS

Laura Vanderkam

(Author & Expert in Time Management)

Laura Vanderkam (born 1978) is an American author and speaker renowned for her expertise in time management and productivity. After graduating from Princeton University, Vanderkam pursued a career in journalism, where she honed her skills in writing about business, careers, and personal development. Her interest in how people spend their time led her to become a leading voice in the field of productivity.

Vanderkam gained widespread recognition with her 2010 book *168 Hours: You Have More Time Than You Think*, which challenges the notion that busy people don't have time for what matters most. Through research and interviews, she reveals strategies that highly successful people use to manage their time effectively. Her follow-up books, including *What the Most Successful People Do Before Breakfast* and *Off the Clock*, further explore how to maximize productivity and live a balanced life.

In addition to her writing, Vanderkam is a sought-after speaker and the co-host of the *Best of Both Worlds* podcast, where she discusses time management strategies for balancing career and family life. Her work has empowered countless individuals to take control of their schedules and achieve their personal and professional goals.

*Book Title

Time is a choice. If we don't like how we're spending an hour, we can choose differently.
—*168 Hours, 2010

We don't build the lives we want by saving time. We build the lives we want, and then time saves itself.
—*Off the Clock, 2018

Break big goals into manageable steps. That way, even if you're tired, overwhelmed, or distracted, you can still make progress.
—Blog post on LauraVanderkam.com, 2019

The key to time management is treating our priorities like they matter.
—*168 Hours, 2010

A successful life is lived in hours, not years.
—*I Know How She Does It, 2015

Instead of saying "I don't have time", try saying "It's not a priority", and see how that feels.
—*168 Hours, 2010

People are remarkably good at making time for what matters once they believe it's possible.
—*168 Hours, 2010

Time freedom isn't about having lots of empty hours; it's about having control over how you spend the hours you have.
—*Off the Clock, 2018

— LAURA VANDERKAM

AUTHORS & EXPERTS

Leo Babauta

(Author & Expert in Productivity)

Leo Babauta (born 1973) is a writer and blogger best known for his work on mindfulness, simplicity, and habit formation. Originally from Guam, Babauta moved to the United States in the early 2000s and began his journey toward a simpler, more intentional life. Struggling with debt, poor health, and busy life demands, he started making small changes that eventually led to profound personal transformation.

In 2007, Babauta launched *Zen Habits*, a blog focused on simplifying life, building positive habits, and cultivating mindfulness. The blog quickly gained a large following, resonating with readers seeking practical advice on how to lead more meaningful lives. His writing, characterized by its simplicity and clarity, offers readers actionable steps to declutter their minds and environments. Babauta's minimalist approach to life, coupled with his practical advice, has inspired millions worldwide to prioritize what truly matters.

Babauta has also authored several books, including *The Power of Less*, in which he outlines the principles of simplicity that have guided his personal and professional life. He continues to write, sharing his insights on living with intention, and remains a prominent voice in the simplicity and mindfulness movements. Babauta's work encourages others to slow down, focus on the essentials, and live more deliberately.

*Book Title

> Simplicity boils down to two steps: Identify the essential. Eliminate the rest.
> —Blog post on Zen Habits, 2008

> The key to changing everything is in the small things, done daily.
> —*The Power of Less, 2009

> Focus on the present, and the future will unfold naturally.
> —Blog post on Zen Habits, 2007

> It's the journey, not the destination, that brings fulfillment.
> —Blog post on Zen Habits, 2010

> You can't do it all. Pick the most important things and let the rest go.
> —*The Power of Less, 2009

> Don't wait for perfection. Start now. Do what you can with what you have.
> —Blog post on Zen Habits, 2007

> Small, simple changes are sustainable and build momentum over time.
> —*The Power of Less, 2009

> By setting limitations, we must choose the essential. So in everything you do, learn to set limitations.
> —*The Power of Less, 2009

> The act of writing things down is one of the most important and powerful tools for prioritizing and planning.
> —Blog post on Zen Habits, 2009

— LEO BABAUTA

AUTHORS & EXPERTS

Marie Kondo

(Author & Expert in Productivity)

Marie Kondo (born 1984) is a Japanese organizing consultant and author best known for her revolutionary tidying-up approach. Kondo began her career as a professional organizer in Tokyo, where she developed the KonMari Method — a unique philosophy that encourages people to keep only items that "spark joy". Her method gained widespread attention with the release of her book, *The Life-Changing Magic of Tidying Up*, which became a global bestseller.

Kondo's influence extended beyond books as she became an international phenomenon with her Netflix series, *Tidying Up with Marie Kondo*, premiered in 2019. The show brought her organizational philosophy into homes around the world, inspiring a cultural shift towards minimalism and mindful living. Her approach focuses on decluttering physical spaces and promotes mental clarity and well-being.

In addition to her media success, Kondo has built a successful business empire, including an online shop and a network of certified KonMari consultants who help others implement her method. Through her work, Kondo has transformed the way people view their belongings and their relationship with material possessions, making her a significant figure in modern lifestyle and productivity movements.

*Book Title

Keep only those things that speak to your heart. Then take the plunge and discard all the rest.
—*The Life-Changing Magic of Tidying Up, 2014

When you tidy your space completely, you transform the scenery of your life.
—*The Life-Changing Magic of Tidying Up, 2014

The question of what you want to own is actually the question of how you want to live your life.
—*The Life-Changing Magic of Tidying Up, 2014

Visible mess helps distract us from the true source of the disorder.
—*The Life-Changing Magic of Tidying Up, 2014

People cannot change their habits without first changing their way of thinking.
—*Spark Joy, 2016

The best way to find out what we really need is to get rid of what we don't.
—*The Life-Changing Magic of Tidying Up, 2014

Letting go is even more important than adding.
—*The Life-Changing Magic of Tidying Up, 2014

Tidying is just a tool, not the final destination. Your real goal should be to establish the lifestyle you want most once your house has been put in order.
—*The Life-Changing Magic of Tidying Up, 2014

— MARIE KONDO

Michael Hyatt

(Author & Expert in Leadership)

Michael Hyatt (born 1955) is a renowned author, speaker, and former CEO, best known for his work in leadership and personal productivity. He began his career in the publishing industry, eventually becoming the CEO of Thomas Nelson Publishers, where he played a crucial role in transforming the company into the world's most prominent Christian publishing house. Under his leadership, Thomas Nelson expanded its reach and influence, publishing numerous bestsellers.

In 2011, Hyatt transitioned from corporate leadership to focus on his passion for helping individuals and organizations achieve their goals. He founded Michael Hyatt & Company, a leadership development firm that provides resources, coaching, and training to professionals. His book *Platform: Get Noticed in a Noisy World* (2012) became a bestseller and is widely regarded as a must-read for anyone looking to build an online presence.

Hyatt's influence extends through his popular podcast, *Lead to Win*, and several other bestselling books, including *Your Best Year Ever* (2018) and *The Vision-Driven Leader* (2020). His work has empowered countless individuals to improve their productivity and leadership skills, making him a respected voice in personal and professional development.

Book Title

What gets scheduled gets done.
—*Your Best Year Ever, 2018

You lose your way when you lose your why.
—The EntreLeadership Podcast, 2014

If you don't have a plan for your life, someone else does.
—*Living Forward, 2016

Focus on your strengths, not your weaknesses.
—Blog post on MichaelHyatt.com, 2015

A goal without a date is just a dream.
—*Your Best Year Ever, 2018

No one ever drifted to a destination they would have chosen.
—*Living Forward, 2016

Success is not how high you've climbed, but how you make a positive difference to the world.
—The Brendon Show podcast, 2016

The most successful people are not those who work longer hours, but those who work smarter.
—Blog post on MichaelHyatt.com, 2018

What you focus on, you become.
—*Your Best Year Ever, 2018

Leaders must understand that results are measured by impact, not hours worked.
—The Michael Hyatt Show, 2017

— MICHAEL HYATT

Michael Porter

(Author & Expert in Strategic Thinking)

Michael Porter (born 1947) is a renowned American academic and economist widely recognized for his influential theories in business strategy. A professor at Harvard Business School, Porter is best known for developing the "Five Forces" framework, a tool that helps businesses analyze their competitive environment. This model has become a foundational concept in the study of competitive strategy, providing insights into market dynamics and industry profitability.

Porter's work extends beyond theory to practical application. In his 1985 book *Competitive Advantage: Creating and Sustaining Superior Performance*, he emphasizes the importance of value chains and strategic positioning in achieving long-term business success. His frameworks are not just theoretical constructs, but practical tools that continue to empower companies to understand how to outperform their rivals by leveraging their strengths and resources.

Beyond business, Porter has contributed to various social issues, including healthcare and economic development. His work on "clusters" highlights the importance of geographic concentrations of industries in driving innovation and economic growth. Porter's ideas remain essential to corporate leaders and policymakers, helping them navigate complex competitive landscapes and foster economic progress.

*Book Title

Strategy is about making choices, trade-offs; it's about deliberately choosing to be different.
—*Harvard Business Review*, 1996

A company without a strategy is willing to try anything.
—*Harvard Business Review*, 1996

The best CEOs I know are teachers, and at the core of what they teach is strategy.
—*Harvard Business Review*, 2014

Sound strategy starts with having the right goal.
—*Harvard Business Review*, 1996

You can't be all things to all people.
—*Competitive Advantage*, 1985

The underlying principles of strategy are enduring, regardless of technology or the pace of change.
—*Harvard Business Review*, 1996

If all you're trying to do is essentially the same thing as your rivals, then it's unlikely that you'll be very successful.
—*Competitive Advantage*, 1985

The key to sustained competitive advantage is to make your strategic positioning sustainable.
—*Harvard Business Review*, 1996

A strategy delineates a territory in which a company seeks to be unique.
—*Harvard Business Review*, 1996

— MICHAEL PORTER

AUTHORS & EXPERTS

Nancy Duarte

(Author & Expert in Communication)

Nancy Duarte (born 1950) is a communication expert and the founder of Duarte, Inc., a leading design and communications firm. She is best known for her groundbreaking work in visual storytelling, helping business leaders and speakers convey their ideas in ways that engage and inspire audiences. Duarte's work has been instrumental in shaping how companies like Apple and Google deliver their messages.

Her most significant contribution came with her book *Slide:ology* (2008), where she laid out practical strategies for creating effective presentations. In *Resonate* (2010), she introduced the concept of applying storytelling techniques to presentations, highlighting the importance of structuring talks with a beginning, middle, and end to connect emotionally with audiences.

Duarte has become a trusted advisor to top executives and organizations, transforming their approaches to public speaking and communication. Her TED Talk on storytelling has reached millions, reinforcing her status as a leader in the field. Through her books, workshops, and firm, she continues to elevate the art of communication.

*Book Title

People don't fall in love with your idea; they fall in love with how your idea affects them.
—*Resonate, 2010*

Great presentations are conversations with your audience, not one-sided speeches.
—*HBR Guide to Persuasive Presentations, 2012*

The greatest communicators have a deep sense of humility and a focus on serving the audience.
—*HBR Guide to Persuasive Presentations, 2012*

Data isn't just numbers. It has a story to tell, and it's your job to give it a voice.
—*DataStory, 2019*

When you create a story with a purpose, you create a presentation that people remember.
—*Resonate, 2010*

Design is a powerful, silent ambassador for your ideas.
—*Slide:ology, 2008*

The greatest way to influence someone is to let them know how much you care about them.
—*Illuminate, 2016*

Speakers must deliver ideas that not only inform but also inspire their audience to take action.
—*Resonate, 2010*

— NANCY DUARTE

Nassim Nicholas Taleb

(Author & Expert in Adaptability)

Nassim Nicholas Taleb (born 1960) is a scholar, statistician, and former trader known for his work on risk, uncertainty, and probability. Born in Lebanon, Taleb has had a diverse career spanning finance, academia, and writing. His early career as a derivatives trader and risk analyst provided practical insight into the unpredictable nature of markets, which shaped much of his later intellectual work.

Taleb's most influential book, *The Black Swan* (2007), introduced the concept of "black swan events"—rare, unpredictable occurrences with massive impact. This idea revolutionized how people think about risk in fields as diverse as finance, economics, and even politics. His book became a bestseller, cemented his reputation as a leading thinker on uncertainty. He further explored these themes in his five-volume series *Incerto*, which includes works like *Antifragile* and *Skin in the Game*.

In addition to his writing, Taleb has held positions at several universities, including New York University, where he has taught risk engineering. His work challenges conventional wisdom about risk management and decision-making, making him a vital voice in debates about finance, business, and navigating an unpredictable world.

*Book Title

The three most harmful addictions are heroin, carbohydrates, and a monthly salary.
—*Skin in the Game, 2018*

Antifragility is beyond resilience or robustness. The resilient resists shocks and stays the same; the antifragile gets better.
—*Antifragile, 2012*

It is much easier to buy and sell than to make products that stay sold.
—*Fooled by Randomness, 2001*

In business and in life, you don't get what you deserve, you get what you negotiate.
—*Antifragile, 2012*

You are rich if and only if money you refuse tastes better than money you accept.
—*The Bed of Procrustes, 2010*

The robust doesn't care; the fragile breaks; the antifragile grows stronger.
—*Antifragile, 2012*

Missing a train is only painful if you run after it! Likewise, not matching the idea of success others expect from you is only painful if that's what you are seeking.
—*The Black Swan, 2007*

The general principle of antifragility, the phenomenon of benefitting from randomness and uncertainty, is of particular relevance in complex systems, where prediction is impossible.
—*Antifragile, 2012*

— NASSIM NICHOLAS TALEB

AUTHORS & EXPERTS

Nick Murray

(Author & Expert in Finance)

Nick Murray (born 1946) is a towering figure in the financial advice industry, renowned for his profound insights into investor behavior and wealth management. His career, which commenced in the late 1960s, has significantly shaped the industry, empowering financial advisors to enhance their practices and better serve their clients. Murray's expertise, firmly grounded in the belief that long-term investing in equities is the most reliable route to wealth, has left an indelible mark on the industry.

Murray's influence is perhaps best encapsulated in his widely acclaimed book *Simple Wealth, Inevitable Wealth*. In this work, he emphasizes the importance of staying invested in the stock market through its ups and downs, urging advisors to instill patience and confidence in their clients. He argues that enduring wealth is built not through market timing or speculation but through a disciplined, long-term approach to investing.

In addition to his writing, Murray is a sought-after speaker and consultant known for his ability to articulate complex financial principles in clear, relatable terms. His monthly newsletter, a resource for financial professionals for many years, offers practical advice and encouragement. Murray's work has left a lasting mark on the industry, helping countless advisors guide their clients to financial security.

Book Title

Timing the market is a fool's game, whereas time in the market is your greatest natural advantage.
—*Simple Wealth, Inevitable Wealth, 1999*

The primary reason for long-term investment success is not brilliance, but patience.
—*Simple Wealth, Inevitable Wealth, 1999*

Successful investing is not about avoiding risk. It's about managing risk.
—*The Excellent Investment Advisor, 1996*

You make most of your money in a bear market; you just don't realize it at the time.
—*Simple Wealth, Inevitable Wealth, 1999*

The only wealth you will ever create is the wealth that will come from the future appreciation of the assets you own today.
—*Simple Wealth, Inevitable Wealth, 1999*

If you can't handle the downside, you don't deserve the upside.
—*Simple Wealth, Inevitable Wealth, 1999*

Volatility is not risk. Risk is the permanent loss of capital.
—*The Excellent Investment Advisor, 1996*

The investor's chief problem—and even his worst enemy—is likely to be himself.
—*The Excellent Investment Advisor, 1996*

The essence of wealth building is to buy great companies and hold them for the long term, regardless of the noise.
—*Simple Wealth, Inevitable Wealth, 1999*

— NICK MURRAY

Peter Drucker

(Author & Expert in Management)

Peter Drucker (1909–2005) was a highly influential management consultant, educator, and author, often regarded as the father of modern management. Born in Austria, he immigrated to the United States in the 1930s, where he developed groundbreaking theories on management and organizational structure. His book *The Practice of Management* (1954) was one of the first to view management as a distinct discipline, shaping how businesses approached leadership and efficiency.

Drucker's ideas transformed how organizations operate. He introduced concepts like "management by objectives", advocating for clear goals and decentralized decision-making. He was also among the first to emphasize the importance of "knowledge workers" and their critical role in the growing post-industrial economy. His consultancy work with major corporations, including General Motors, brought his theories into practice on a large scale.

Throughout his career, Drucker authored over 30 books on management, economics, and society, continuing to influence generations of business leaders. His emphasis on innovation, adaptability, and social responsibility helped shape the modern business landscape. Drucker's teachings remain a cornerstone of business education, inspiring companies to focus not just on profits but on contributing positively to society.

*Book Title

The best way to predict the future is to create it.
—*Management, 1973*

Management is doing things right; leadership is doing the right things.
—*The Essential Drucker, 2001*

What gets measured gets managed.
—*Management Challenges for the 21st Century, 1999*

There is nothing so useless as doing efficiently that which should not be done at all.
—*The Effective Executive, 1967*

The purpose of a business is to create and keep a customer.
—*The Practice of Management, 1954*

Plans are only good intentions unless they immediately degenerate into hard work.
—*The Effective Executive, 1967*

If you want something new, you have to stop doing something old.
—*Managing for Results, 1964*

Time is the scarcest resource, and unless it is managed, nothing else can be managed.
—*The Effective Executive, 1967*

The entrepreneur always searches for change, responds to it, and exploits it as an opportunity.
—*Innovation and Entrepreneurship, 1985*

— PETER DRUCKER

Peter Senge

(Author & Expert in Organizational Theory)

Peter Senge (born 1947) is a systems scientist and organizational theorist known for his work on leadership and learning organizations. He earned a PhD in Management from the MIT Sloan School of Management and is a senior lecturer at MIT. Senge's early academic work focused on systems thinking, a holistic approach to understanding complex systems, which would later form the basis of his influential theories.

Senge's most notable contribution is his 1990 book, *The Fifth Discipline: The Art and Practice of the Learning Organization*. In it, he introduced the "learning organization" concept, where employees continually expand their capacity to achieve their goals, fostering a culture of continuous learning and adaptability. His work emphasizes five key disciplines: personal mastery, mental models, shared vision, team learning, and systems thinking, with systems thinking being the "fifth discipline" that integrates the others.

A thought leader in organizational development, Senge's ideas have impacted business strategy, leadership, and innovation. His work has encouraged companies to rethink traditional management models and embrace more collaborative, flexible structures that promote long-term success. He continues influencing fields such as education, sustainability, and leadership development.

*Book Title

Learning organizations are organizations where people continually expand their capacity to create the results they truly desire.
—*The Fifth Discipline, 1990*

The only sustainable competitive advantage is an organization's ability to learn faster than the competition.
—*The Fifth Discipline, 1990*

People don't resist change. They resist being changed.
—*The Dance of Change, 1999*

Systems thinking is a discipline for seeing wholes. It is a framework for seeing interrelationships rather than things, for seeing patterns of change rather than static "snapshots".
—*The Fifth Discipline, 1990*

Today's problems come from yesterday's "solutions".
—*The Fifth Discipline, 1990*

A shared vision is not an idea... it is rather, a force in people's hearts, a force of impressive power.
—*The Fifth Discipline, 1990*

You cannot force commitment, what you can do... You nudge a little here, inspire a little there, and provide a role model. Commitment is self-generated.
—*The Fifth Discipline, 1990*

Mental models are deeply ingrained assumptions, generalizations, or even pictures or images that influence how we understand the world and how we take action.
—*The Fifth Discipline, 1990*

— PETER SENGE

Philip Kotler

(Author & Expert in Marketing)

Philip Kotler (born 1931) is an American marketing expert, often regarded as the father of modern marketing. He earned his PhD in economics from the Massachusetts Institute of Technology (MIT) and later shifted his focus to marketing, revolutionizing the field with his innovative theories. Kotler is a Distinguished Professor of International Marketing at the Kellogg School of Management, Northwestern University, where he has influenced generations of marketers.

Kotler's groundbreaking book, *Marketing Management*, first published in 1967, became a foundational text in the discipline and remains one of the most widely used marketing textbooks globally. His marketing approach emphasized customer needs, value creation, and the importance of strategic marketing in long-term business success. He introduced the concept of social marketing and was one of the first to explore the intersection of marketing and societal impact.

In addition to his academic work, Kotler has consulted for leading global companies such as IBM, General Electric, and Michelin, helping them craft strategies to adapt to changing markets. His thought leadership continues to shape how businesses understand market dynamics, making him one of the most influential figures in marketing and business strategy.

Book Title

Marketing is not the art of finding clever ways to dispose of what you make. It is the art of creating genuine customer value.
—*According to Kotler, 2005*

The aim of marketing is to know and understand the customer so well the product or service fits him and sells itself.
—*Marketing Insights from A to Z, 2003*

The best advertising is done by satisfied customers.
—*Marketing Insights from A to Z, 2003*

Marketing takes a day to learn. Unfortunately, it takes a lifetime to master.
—*Marketing Insights from A to Z, 2003*

Your company does not belong in markets where it cannot be the best.
—*According to Kotler, 2005*

A good company offers excellent products and services. A great company also offers excellent products and services but also strives to make the world a better place.
—*Marketing 3.0, 2010*

Good companies will meet needs; great companies will create markets.
—*Marketing 3.0, 2010*

Authenticity, honesty, and personal voice underlie much of what's successful on the Web.
—*Marketing Insights from A to Z, 2003*

— PHILIP KOTLER

Porter Gale

(Author & Expert in Networking)

Porter Gale (born 1964) is a marketing expert, author, and entrepreneur, widely recognized for her role as the former Vice President of Marketing at Virgin America. While at Virgin America, she was instrumental in shaping the brand's identity, focusing on customer experience and innovative digital marketing strategies. Her work helped turn the airline into a beloved brand, known for its loyal customer base and modern approach to air travel.

Gale is also the author of *Your Network is Your Net Worth*, which explores the power of relationships in personal and professional success. She emphasizes how networking can lead to opportunities and growth when done with authenticity and intention. This concept has become central to her teachings on business development and personal branding.

In addition to her marketing career, Gale has advised startups and invested in emerging businesses. She is a sought-after speaker on topics related to entrepreneurship, marketing, and the importance of building meaningful connections. Gale's work continues to inspire business leaders to focus on relationships and authenticity as core drivers of long-term success.

*Book Title

Your network is your net worth.
—*Your Network Is Your Net Worth, 2013*

Opportunities do not float like clouds in the sky. They are attached to people.
—*Your Network Is Your Net Worth, 2013*

Relationships are the currency of power, influence, and success.
—*Forbes, 2013*

When you help others, you help yourself.
—*Your Network Is Your Net Worth, 2013*

Networking is not about just connecting people. It's about connecting people with people, people with ideas, and people with opportunities.
—*Speech at TEDx San Francisco, 2013*

Passion projects lead to networking success because passion attracts attention and ignites creativity.
—*Your Network Is Your Net Worth, 2013*

When you change your mindset, you change your outcomes.
—*Blog post on PorterGale.com, 2013*

In business, the most powerful assets you can have are relationships built on trust.
—*Your Network Is Your Net Worth, 2013*

You are the average of the five people you spend the most time with.
—*Huffington Post, 2013*

— PORTER GALE

AUTHORS & EXPERTS

Ramit Sethi

(Author & Expert in Finance)

Ramit Sethi (born 1982) is an American personal finance advisor, entrepreneur, and author best known for his practical approach to wealth-building. He gained prominence with his 2009 book, *I Will Teach You to Be Rich*, which became a New York Times bestseller. The book, which provides actionable strategies for managing money, investing, and optimizing personal finances, resonated with a young audience looking to gain control over their financial lives.

Sethi's journey into personal finance began while studying psychology at Stanford University, where he developed a deep interest in behavioral economics. This led him to create a blog in 2004, sharing tips on saving, investing, and living a financially conscious life. His straightforward and sometimes unconventional advice, combined with a focus on automating finances, has helped many readers and followers build wealth over time.

In addition to his writing, Sethi founded GrowthLab and I Will Teach You to Be Rich, Inc., which offer online courses on earning more money, starting businesses, and mastering one's psychology around finances. Through his work, Sethi has influenced millions to take control of their financial future, emphasizing that a "rich life" is not just about money but about using it to live a life you love.

*Book Title

Focus on the big wins: automation, investing early, negotiating a higher salary, and earning more—not on cutting $3 lattes.
—*I Will Teach You to Be Rich, 2009

There's a limit to how much you can cut, but there's no limit to how much you can earn.
—CNBC, 2019

Spend extravagantly on the things you love, and cut costs mercilessly on the things you don't.
—*I Will Teach You to Be Rich, 2009

Success isn't about taking risks blindly; it's about taking calculated risks.
—Business Insider, 2017

People who get rich think about the long term—they invest in skills, relationships, and assets that grow over time.
—Entrepreneur, 2016

Your financial life is more about the systems you use than the products you buy.
—The Dave Ramsey Show, 2019

The rich don't only focus on saving—they focus on earning more.
—Podcast The Tony Robbins Show, 2017

Your rich life is yours alone. It's the life you want to live, funded by your money, not someone else's idea of what you should do.
—*I Will Teach You to Be Rich, 2009

— RAMIT SETHI

Robert Kiyosaki

(Author & Expert in Finance)

Robert Kiyosaki (born 1947) is an entrepreneur, educator, and author best known for his book *Rich Dad Poor Dad*, which has become a classic in personal finance literature. Born in Hilo, Hawaii, Kiyosaki served in the U.S. Marine Corps during the Vietnam War before starting a business career. His experiences shaped his views on money and financial education, leading him to advocate for financial literacy as a key to achieving financial independence.

Kiyosaki's most significant achievement is the *Rich Dad* series, starting with *Rich Dad Poor Dad* in 1997. The book contrasts the financial philosophies of his two "dads"— his biological father and the father of his best friend — illustrating the difference between traditional beliefs about money and those that lead to wealth creation. The book has inspired millions worldwide to rethink their approach to money, emphasizing the importance of assets, entrepreneurship, and passive income.

Beyond writing, Kiyosaki has founded several companies and developed educational products focused on financial literacy. His board game, *Cashflow*, teaches players how to invest and manage money, reflecting his belief that practical experience is the best teacher. Kiyosaki's influence extends globally, inspiring people to take control of their financial futures.

*Book Title

If you want to go somewhere, it is best to find someone who has already been there.
—*Rich Dad's Guide to Investing, 2000*

Don't let the fear of losing be greater than the excitement of winning.
—*Rich Dad Poor Dad, 1997*

It's not how much money you make, but how much money you keep, how hard it works for you, and how many generations you keep it for.
—*Rich Dad Poor Dad, 1997*

The single most powerful asset we all have is our mind. If it is trained well, it can create enormous wealth.
—*Rich Dad Poor Dad, 1997*

The size of your success is measured by the strength of your desire, the size of your dream, and how you handle disappointment along the way.
—*Retire Young Retire Rich, 2002*

The most successful people in life are the ones who ask questions. They're always learning. They're always growing. They're always pushing.
—*Rich Dad's Guide to Investing, 2000*

Your future is created by what you do today, not tomorrow.
—*The Real Book of Real Estate, 2009*

The poor and the middle-class work for money. The rich have money work for them.
—*Rich Dad Poor Dad, 1997*

— ROBERT KIYOSAKI

Robin Sharma

(Author & Expert in Leadership)

Robin Sharma (born 1964) is a Canadian writer and leadership expert, best known for his bestselling book *The Monk Who Sold His Ferrari*. Originally a lawyer, Sharma left his legal career to focus on personal development and leadership coaching, a decision that transformed him into one of the field's most sought-after speakers and authors.

Sharma's breakthrough came with the publication of *The Monk Who Sold His Ferrari* in 1997, a fable that intertwines spiritual wisdom with practical life lessons. The book's success led to a series of influential works, including *The Leader Who Had No Title*, which emphasizes the importance of leadership at all levels, regardless of official rank. His teachings are widely respected by global leaders and Fortune 500 companies, who seek his advice on leadership, productivity, and personal mastery.

In addition to his writing, Sharma has delivered keynote speeches worldwide and founded Sharma Leadership International, a training firm dedicated to helping organizations develop world-class leaders. His work inspires millions to pursue excellence, live purposefully, and achieve success through inner growth and disciplined practice.

*Book Title

Dream big. Start small. Act now.
—*The 5 AM Club, 2018*

The smallest of actions is always better than the noblest of intentions.
—*The Leader Who Had No Title, 2010*

The only limits on your life are the ones that you set yourself.
—*The Monk Who Sold His Ferrari, 1997*

Your "I CAN" is more important than your IQ.
—*The Leader Who Had No Title, 2010*

What you focus on grows, what you think about expands, and what you dwell upon determines your destiny.
—*The Monk Who Sold His Ferrari, 1997*

Your excuses are nothing more than the lies your fears have sold you.
—*The Greatness Guide, 2006*

The secret to genius is not genetics but daily practice married with relentless perseverance.
—*The Monk Who Sold His Ferrari, 1997*

If you want to be extraordinary, be prepared to do what ordinary people are not willing to do.
—*The 5 AM Club, 2018*

Don't live the same year 75 times and call it a life.
—*The Greatness Guide, 2006*

— ROBIN SHARMA

Roger Fisher

(Author & Expert in Negotiation)

Roger Fisher (1922–2012) was a renowned expert in negotiation and conflict resolution, best known for shaping modern negotiation theory. After serving as a pilot in World War II, he earned a law degree from Harvard, where he would later become a professor. His early career included time as a lawyer and government advisor, but his work in diplomacy and negotiation defined his legacy.

Fisher co-authored *Getting to Yes* in 1981, a groundbreaking book that introduced "principled negotiation". This method focuses on separating people from the problem and finding mutual interests to reach agreements that benefit all parties. His approach to negotiation has been adopted in business, law, and international diplomacy, making him a global thought leader in the field.

Beyond his academic contributions, Fisher was deeply involved in real-world negotiations, advising on peace talks and high-stakes disputes around the world. He founded the Harvard Negotiation Project, which continues to develop strategies for resolving conflicts. Fisher's work has left an enduring impact on how organizations and individuals approach negotiation and problem-solving.

*Book Title

The ability to see the situation as the other side sees it is one of the most important skills a negotiator can possess.
—*Getting to Yes, 1981*

Negotiation is not a zero-sum game; both sides can win if they approach it collaboratively.
—*Getting to Yes, 1981*

The key to successful negotiation is separating the people from the problem.
—*Getting to Yes, 1981*

The best way to handle a conflict is not to argue over positions, but to focus on underlying interests.
—*Getting to Yes, 1981*

The only way to get the best of an argument is to avoid it.
—*Beyond Machiavelli, 1994*

In business negotiations, the wise person learns to ask, not to tell.
—*Getting It Done, 1994*

It's not enough to have an answer. You need to have a good reason for why your answer is right.
—*Getting to Yes, 1981*

A successful negotiation is when both parties feel they've gained something.
—*Getting to Yes, 1981*

— ROGER FISHER

Seth Godin

(Author & Expert in Marketing)

Seth Godin (born 1960) is an American entrepreneur, author, and marketing expert renowned for his insights on modern marketing, leadership, and creativity. After earning an MBA from Stanford University, he began his career in publishing but soon moved into the digital space, founding Yoyodyne, one of the first internet-based direct marketing companies, which was acquired by Yahoo! in 1998.

Godin has written over 20 books, many of which have become bestsellers, including *Purple Cow* and *Linchpin*. His work emphasizes the importance of standing out in a crowded market by being remarkable, building trust with customers, and focusing on long-term relationships rather than short-term sales. His concept of "permission marketing" revolutionized the way companies think about customer engagement, advocating for marketing that customers opt into, rather than interruptive advertising.

Beyond his writing, Godin is a sought-after speaker and the creator of one of the most popular marketing blogs in the world. He also launched the AltMBA, an online leadership and management workshop that has trained professionals globally. Godin has influenced how individuals and companies approach marketing, creativity, and business in the digital age through his books, blog, and educational initiatives.

*Book Title

People do not buy goods and services. They buy relations, stories, and magic.
—*The Cluetrain Manifesto, 1999*

The cost of being wrong is less than the cost of doing nothing.
—*The Dip, 2007*

Marketing is no longer about the stuff that you make but about the stories you tell.
—*All Marketers Are Liars, 2009*

Don't find customers for your products, find products for your customers.
—*Permission Marketing, 1999*

If it scares you, it might be a good thing to try.
—*Linchpin, 2010*

The secret to leadership is simple: Do what you believe in. Paint a picture of the future. Go there. People will follow.
—*Tribes, 2011*

The only way to be indispensable is to be different.
—*Linchpin, 2010*

You don't need more time, you just need to decide.
—The Linchpin Manifesto, 2010

How dare you settle for less when the world has made it so easy for you to be remarkable?
—*Purple Cow, 2003*

— SETH GODIN

Simon Sinek

(Author & Expert in Leadership)

Simon Sinek (born 1973) is a British-American author and motivational speaker best known for his work on leadership and inspiration in business. He gained international recognition with his 2009 TED Talk, *How Great Leaders Inspire Action*, which introduced his concept of "The Golden Circle". This framework explains how successful leaders and organizations start with "why", a purpose or belief that drives them, rather than focusing solely on "what" they do or "how" they do it.

Sinek's bestselling book *Start With Why* (2009) expanded on this idea, exploring the power of purpose-driven leadership. He followed it with *Leaders Eat Last* (2014), which focuses on the importance of trust, empathy, and collaboration in creating successful teams. His work has been adopted by corporations, non-profits, and military organizations seeking to foster innovation and improve leadership practices.

Sinek has become a sought-after speaker and consultant, working with major organizations like Microsoft and the United Nations. His books, including *The Infinite Game* (2019), continue to shape modern discussions on leadership, culture, and strategy. They emphasize long-term thinking and resilience in business. His transformative ideas encourage leaders to inspire rather than manipulate, creating environments where people feel valued and purpose driven.

*Book Title

People don't buy what you do; they buy why you do it.
—*Start with Why, 2009

Working hard for something we don't care about is called stress; working hard for something we love is called passion.
—Keynote Speech at Live2Lead, 2014

Leadership is not about being in charge. It's about taking care of those in your charge.
—*Leaders Eat Last, 2014

Great companies don't hire skilled people and motivate them; they hire already motivated people and inspire them.
—*Start with Why, 2009

There are only two ways to influence human behavior: you can manipulate it, or you can inspire it.
—*Start with Why, 2009

A team is not a group of people who work together. A team is a group of people who trust each other.
—*Leaders Eat Last, 2014

If you hire people just because they can do a job, they'll work for your money. But if you hire people who believe what you believe, they'll work for you with blood, sweat, and tears.
—*Start with Why, 2009

Success is when reality catches up to your imagination.
—Interview with LinkedIn Influencers, 2015

— SIMON SINEK

Stephen Covey

(Author & Expert in Leadership)

Stephen Covey (1932-2012) was an influential American author, educator, and businessman, best known for his seminal work, *The 7 Habits of Highly Effective People*. Born in Salt Lake City, Utah, Covey earned an MBA from Harvard and a Doctor of Religious Education from Brigham Young University. His educational background laid the foundation for his lifelong dedication to leadership and personal development.

Covey's breakthrough came in 1989 with the publication of *The 7 Habits of Highly Effective People*, a book that quickly became a cornerstone of modern self-help literature. Individuals, organizations, and leaders across the globe have widely adopted the book's practical approach to personal and professional effectiveness. Covey's work emphasized principles such as proactivity, goal-setting, and empathic communication, reshaping how people approach personal and professional growth.

Aside from his literary pursuits, Covey played a pivotal role as a co-founder of FranklinCovey, a professional services firm specializing in training and consulting. This venture further solidified his influence in the business world. His teachings, which continue to inspire millions, remain pertinent in the realms of leadership, time management, and personal effectiveness. Covey's legacy lives on through his books, teachings, and the profound impact he had on the lives of countless individuals and organizations.

*Book Title

> The key is not to prioritize what's on your schedule, but to schedule your priorities.
> —*The 7 Habits of Highly Effective People, 1989*

> Most people do not listen with the intent to understand; they listen with the intent to reply.
> —*The 7 Habits of Highly Effective People, 1989*

> Seek first to understand, then to be understood.
> —*The 7 Habits of Highly Effective People, 1989*

> Effective leadership is putting first things first. Effective management is discipline, carrying it out.
> —*The 7 Habits of Highly Effective People, 1989*

> Management is efficiency in climbing the ladder of success; leadership determines whether the ladder is leaning against the right wall.
> —*The 7 Habits of Highly Effective People, 1989*

> You have to decide what your highest priorities are and have the courage—pleasantly, smilingly, non-apologetically—to say "no" to other things.
> —*First Things First, 1994*

> Trust is the glue of life. It's the most essential ingredient in effective communication. It's the foundational principle that holds all relationships.
> —*The 7 Habits of Highly Effective People, 1989*

> I am not a product of my circumstances. I am a product of my decisions.
> —*The 7 Habits of Highly Effective People, 1989*

— STEPHEN COVEY

Suze Orman

(Author & Expert in Finance)

Suze Orman (born 1951) is a prominent financial advisor, author, and television host recognized for her practical advice on personal finance, especially for women. Born in Chicago, Illinois, Orman began her career as a waitress before becoming a financial advisor at Merrill Lynch. Her early struggles with money motivated her to empower others to take control of their finances, establishing her financial planning firm in 1987.

Orman's most significant achievements include her best-selling books and her long-running television program, *The Suze Orman Show*, which aired on CNBC for over a decade. Through books like *The 9 Steps to Financial Freedom* and *Women & Money*, Orman has educated millions on topics such as saving, investing, and retirement planning. Her advice, often focused on financial independence and security, has not only resonated particularly with women seeking to take charge of their financial futures but also inspired them to do so.

Beyond her writing and broadcasting, Orman has influenced public discourse on financial literacy. She has strongly advocated for emergency funds, smart investing, and careful retirement planning, consistently emphasizing the importance of making informed financial decisions. Orman's work has made her a trusted voice in personal finance, inspiring countless individuals to achieve economic stability.

*Book Title

True generosity is an offering; given freely and out of pure love. No strings attached. No expectations.
—*The Courage to Be Rich, 1999*

You need to learn to control your money, or the lack of it will forever control you.
—*The Money Book for the Young, Fabulous & Broke, 2005*

It's better to do nothing with your money than something you don't understand.
—*Suze Orman's Financial Guidebook, 2006*

A big part of financial freedom is having your heart and mind free from worry about the "what-ifs" of life.
—*The 9 Steps to Financial Freedom, 1997*

The most important quality for an investor is temperament, not intellect.
—*The Money Class, 2011*

Debt is bondage. It is a powerful, extraordinarily cruel financial force that will take a lifetime to master.
—*The 9 Steps to Financial Freedom, 1997*

In all realms of life, it takes courage to stretch your limits, express your power, and fulfill your potential.
—*The Courage to Be Rich, 1999*

No one ever achieved financial security by being weak and scared. Confidence and courage are the real tools for business success.
—*The Laws of Money, The Lessons of Life, 2003*

— SUZE ORMAN

Tim Brown

(Author & Expert in Innovation)

Tim Brown (born 1950) is a British industrial designer best known for his influential role as CEO of IDEO, a global design firm that helped popularize the concept of design thinking. After studying at Northumbria University, Brown began his career in product design. Still, it was at IDEO that he truly made his mark by advancing human-centered design methods across industries.

Under Brown's leadership, IDEO transformed design thinking into a strategy for innovation, emphasizing empathy, rapid prototyping, and collaboration. His 2009 book, *Change by Design,* laid out how these principles could be applied beyond product design to areas such as business strategy and social challenges. Companies around the world have adopted these ideas to foster creativity and solve complex problems.

Brown has been a strong advocate for using design thinking to address global issues, including healthcare and education. His contributions have reshaped how businesses and organizations approach innovation, focusing on users' needs and creating sustainable solutions. Even after stepping down as IDEO's CEO, he remains an influential figure in design and continues to promote the role of creativity in driving business success.

*Book Title

Design thinking is a human-centered approach to innovation that draws from the designer's toolkit to integrate the needs of people, the possibilities of technology, and the requirements for business success.
—*Change by Design, 2009

The mission of design thinking is to translate observation into insights, and insights into products and services that will improve lives.
—The New York Times, 2009

Innovation happens when people are given the freedom to ask questions and the resources and power to find the answers.
—Fast Company, 2010

Creativity is not the miraculous road to business growth and affluence that everyone wants it to be, but it can be a significant, practical road if it is approached as a process that anyone can learn and practice.
—*Change by Design, 2009

Design is about the balance between form and function, but also about the balance between art and business.
—TED Talk on Design Thinking, 2009

The design process is about imagining the future, not simply reworking the past.
—*Change by Design, 2009

A prototype is worth a thousand meetings.
—Wired, 2011

— TIM BROWN

AUTHORS & EXPERTS

Tim Ferriss

(Author & Expert in Time Management)

Tim Ferriss (born 1977) is an American author, entrepreneur, and public speaker known for his influence in the self-help and productivity spaces. After studying East Asian Studies at Princeton, he started his career in tech before founding his own company, BrainQUICKEN, which he later sold.

Ferriss' 2007 book *The 4-Hour Workweek* was a game-changer, challenging traditional work norms and advocating for lifestyle design that maximizes freedom and efficiency. Its success not only made Ferriss a best-selling author but also a key figure in the "life-hacking" movement, where he continued to build his brand around optimizing health, productivity, and personal growth.

He is also the host of *The Tim Ferriss Show*, a podcast where he interviews high achievers from various fields. Through is work, Ferriss has become a prominent figure in modern entrepreneurial culture, known for his practical tips on productivity, business, and living a more balanced life.

*Book Title

Focus on being productive instead of busy.
—*The 4-Hour Workweek, 2007

What we fear doing most is usually what we most need to do.
—*The 4-Hour Workweek, 2007

The question you should be asking isn't, "What do I want?" or "What are my goals?" but "What would excite me?"
—*The 4-Hour Workweek, 2007

If you are insecure, guess what? The rest of the world is, too. Do not overestimate the competition and underestimate yourself. You are better than you think.
—*The 4-Hour Workweek, 2007

The goal is not to simply eliminate the bad, but to pursue and experience the best in the world.
—*The 4-Hour Workweek, 2007

A person's success in life can usually be measured by the number of uncomfortable conversations he or she is willing to have.
—*The 4-Hour Workweek, 2007

To enjoy life, you don't need fancy nonsense, but you do need to control your time and realize that most things just aren't as serious as you make them out to be.
—*The 4-Hour Workweek, 2007

"Someday" is a disease that will take your dreams to the grave with you.
—*The 4-Hour Workweek, 2007

— TIM FERRISS

AUTHORS & EXPERTS

Tony Hsieh

(Author & Expert in Customer Focus)

Tony Hsieh (1973–2020) was an entrepreneur best known for transforming Zappos into an online retail giant and revolutionizing customer service. After graduating from Harvard, Hsieh co-founded the advertising network LinkExchange, which he sold to Microsoft in 1998. He then became the CEO of Zappos in 1999, guiding the company through rapid growth by prioritizing customer satisfaction and company culture.

Under Hsieh's leadership, Zappos became a model for employee engagement and innovation. He famously introduced the idea of paying employees to quit, ensuring only those deeply committed to the company stayed on. In 2009, he sold Zappos to Amazon yet remained committed to preserving its unique culture.

Hsieh was also the author of *Delivering Happiness* (2010), which shared his business philosophy centered on happiness and purpose as drivers of success. Outside of Zappos, Hsieh was deeply involved in urban revitalization efforts in Las Vegas, investing in projects to create a vibrant tech and arts community. His legacy is one of visionary leadership, blending financial success with a commitment to human well-being.

Book Title

Customer service shouldn't just be a department, it should be the entire company.
—*Delivering Happiness, 2010*

Chase the vision, not the money; the money will end up following you.
—*Delivering Happiness, 2010*

Your personal core values define who you are, and a company's core values ultimately define the company's character and brand.
—*Delivering Happiness, 2010*

Our belief is that if you get the culture right, most of the other stuff, like great customer service or building a great long-term brand, will happen naturally.
—*Delivering Happiness, 2010*

Don't play games that you don't understand, even if you see lots of other people making money from them.
—*Delivering Happiness, 2010*

Envision, create, and believe in your own universe, and the universe will form around you.
—*Delivering Happiness, 2010*

Have fun. The game is a lot more enjoyable when you're trying to do more than just make money.
—*Delivering Happiness, 2010*

The best businesses are really ones that can combine passion, profits, and purpose.
—*Delivering Happiness, 2010*

— TONY HSIEH

Tony Robbins

(Author & Expert in Growth Mindset)

Tony Robbins (born 1960) is a renowned American life coach, author, and philanthropist, recognized for his personal development and self-help work. His journey from a challenging environment in California to becoming a transformational figure is a testament to the power of positive thinking and strategic planning. His early exposure to motivational speaking through mentor Jim Rohn set the stage for his career.

Robbins gained prominence in the 1980s with his infomercials and self-help books, mainly *Awaken the Giant Within* and *Unlimited Power*, which provided practical techniques for achieving personal and professional goals. His live seminars, such as "Unleash the Power Within", have attracted millions of participants globally, where he emphasizes the importance of mindset, emotional mastery, and financial freedom.

Beyond his motivational work, Robbins has diversified into business and philanthropy. He has advised leaders and celebrities, and through his Tony Robbins Foundation, he has impacted the lives of countless individuals by addressing issues like hunger and education. Robbins' influence extends beyond his seminars and books, making him a pivotal figure in self-improvement and empowerment.

*Book Title

The path to success is to take massive, determined action.
—*Awaken the Giant Within, 1991*

Setting goals is the first step in turning the invisible into the visible.
—*Unlimited Power, 1986*

It's not what we do once in a while that shapes our lives. It's what we do consistently.
—*Awaken the Giant Within, 1991*

Success is doing what you want, when you want, where you want, with whom you want, as much as you want.
—Seminar *Unleash the Power Within, 2007*

If you do what you've always done, you'll get what you've always gotten.
—Seminar *Unleash the Power Within, 2003*

Leaders spend 5% of their time on the problem and 95% of their time on the solution. Get over it and crush it!
—Seminar *Business Mastery, 2010*

People are not lazy. They simply have impotent goals—that is, goals that do not inspire them.
—*Unlimited Power, 1986*

The secret of success is learning how to use pain and pleasure instead of having pain and pleasure use you.
—*Awaken the Giant Within, 1991*

The quality of your life is the quality of your relationships.
—Seminar *Date with Destiny, 1999*

— TONY ROBBINS

Zig Ziglar

(Author & Expert in Sales)

Zig Ziglar (1926–2012) was a renowned American author, salesman, and motivational speaker. He was famous for his dynamic speeches and inspirational messages on success and personal development. Raised in a large family in rural Mississippi during the Great Depression, Ziglar's humble beginnings shaped his work ethic and belief in perseverance. After serving in the Navy during World War II, he began a career in sales, where he quickly excelled, ultimately becoming a top-tier motivational speaker.

Ziglar's most significant contribution came through his books and seminars, where he emphasized positive thinking, goal-setting, and self-discipline. His best-selling book, *See You at the Top*, published in 1974, became a staple in the self-help genre, helping millions achieve personal and professional success. Ziglar's engaging style and memorable quotes, like "You can have everything in life you want if you will just help enough other people get what they want" cemented his reputation as a master motivator.

Throughout his career, Ziglar delivered over 5,000 speeches worldwide, inspiring audiences with his practical wisdom and contagious optimism. His impact extended beyond business, as he focused on holistic success—encompassing family, faith, and personal growth—making him a lasting figure in motivation and leadership.

*Book Title

You don't have to be great to start, but you have to start to be great.
—*Success for Dummies, 2002*

Your attitude, not your aptitude, will determine your altitude.
—*See You at the Top, 1994*

You can have everything in life you want, if you will just help other people get what they want.
—*See You at the Top, 1994*

People often say that motivation doesn't last. Well, neither does bathing—that's why we recommend it daily.
—*Over the Top, 1998*

Expect the best. Prepare for the worst. Capitalize on what comes.
—*Zig Ziglar's Life Lifters, 2000*

Lack of direction, not lack of time, is the problem. We all have twenty-four hour days.
—*Better Than Good, 2007*

When obstacles arise, you change your direction to reach your goal; you do not change your decision to get there.
—*See You at the Top, 1994*

Profitability comes from loyalty, productivity, and having a character base from which to work.
—*Ziglar on Selling, 1998*

If you aim at nothing, you will hit it every time.
—*Over the Top, 1998*

— ZIG ZIGLAR

A HEARTFELT THANK YOU

Success is getting what you want. Happiness is wanting what you get.

— DALE CARNEGIE

A HEARTFELT THANK YOU

Dear Reader,

Thank you for choosing *THE EMPIRIC MBA*. Your decision to learn from the experience of some of the most extraordinary business minds is truly appreciated. I hope that the insights and inspiration you've gained from the stories and quotes of these iconic figures will enrich your journey and empower you to reach new heights in your endeavors.

Writing this book has been a labor of love, and I sincerely hope it serves as a valuable resource in your pursuit. Your feedback is incredibly important to me. If you found this book helpful, I would be grateful if you could take a moment to share your thoughts by leaving a review on Amazon. Your review not only helps me continue to improve but also helps others who are seeking guidance and inspiration.

Thank you once again for your support and for being a part of this amazing adventure. I wish you continued success and fulfillment as you apply the lessons contained within these pages to your own path.

With gratitude,

Mike Vermilion

www.ingramcontent.com/pod-product-compliance
Lightning Source LLC
Chambersburg PA
CBHW031619210526
45464CB00004B/1651